Present in Every Place?

Present in Every Place?

The Church of England and the Parish Vocation

Will Foulger

scm press

© Will Foulger 2023
Published in 2023 by SCM Press
Editorial office
3rd Floor, Invicta House,
108–114 Golden Lane,
London EC1Y 0TG, UK

www.scmpress.co.uk

SCM Press is an imprint of Hymns Ancient & Modern Ltd
(a registered charity)

Hymns Ancient & Modern® is a registered trademark of
Hymns Ancient & Modern Ltd
13A Hellesdon Park Road, Norwich,
Norfolk NR6 5DR, UK

British Library Cataloguing in Publication data
A catalogue record for this book is available
from the British Library

ISBN 978-0-334-06203-5

Typeset by Regent Typesetting
Printed and bound in Great Britain by
CPI Group (UK) Ltd

For my Godfather, Roger.
Who gave me Proverbs 15.17.

Contents

Acknowledgements

I wish to offer thanks to all those who have supported and encouraged me in the writing of this book. The ideas presented here arose out of research I carried out with four very different Church of England churches in four very different places. So the first thank you is for them. Thank you for allowing me to share some small part of your life together, and for letting me see how your worship of Christ led you to love your places.

Thank you to Mum and Dad, and family and friends, all of whom have been more confident about something like this than I have been.

To my colleagues at Cranmer Hall who have been a source not only of theological insight and questioning but also laughter. A particular thank you to Philip Plyming, who encouraged me to be here doing this, and who has made things work so that I have had space to think and write. Thanks, Sam, for reading some of this and for sparking ideas. Thanks go too to Robert Song and Alan Bartlett, my doctoral supervisors and the ones who planted the seed of an idea that would become this book. And to all my theology teachers over the years who have had a part in shaping these reflections. I mention here especially Alan Torrance, who first instilled in me a hunger to know more about the God who is free. That has remained my theological instinct all these years, and I will be forever grateful. Thank you to my friends in Nottingham – and at Trinity Church in particular – where I was privileged to see that all this might really matter.

To everyone at SCM Press who has made this such an easy process to be a part of, thank you. And especially to David

Shervington, for first opening the door of possibility and then for carrying it through to where we are now.

The final thank you must go to my family. Vikki and Iris, Joe, Jesse and Huck have been patient with me as I have juggled demands. What I said back then is truer now than ever: you make everywhere that we are a place I want to belong.

Preface

This is a book about churches and the places they have been given to love. It is about old churches and new churches and what they might have in common. It is about the Church of England and the idea that, within the economy of God, this small part of the body of Christ may have a particular charism – a gift. It is about what it might mean to say that the Church of England has a vocation to be present in the places of the nation; the cure of souls for every person and community within the place they sit. It is about what such a vocation might mean today and whether it has any purchase on the realities of the world we live in. It is about how we take what we have received and make sense of it in the present. And it is about how we might talk all this through together, as one church.

One feature of place is that its future is wedded to its past: you have to go back to go forward. So allow me to go back in the story of this book as a means to outline the direction of travel for what follows. The book originates in some research I carried out with four Church of England churches back in 2014–16. I set out then with the intention of defending the new churches (fresh expressions, church plants etc.) from many of the theological criticisms that had been levelled against them. I chose as my research churches two fresh expressions and two parish churches within the same diocese. My goal was to spend time with the churches, exploring how they interacted with their local places, and hopefully showing that the picture on the ground was more sophisticated than the critics ('parish or no parish?!') supposed. The problem arose, however, that the more I read the critics, then the more I found myself agreeing with their premises. I was especially drawn to this idea of place, on which they relied heavily. That there is a difference between being rooted geographically and living as if you could avoid it. That the parish is significant because – so the argument goes – it grounds a church in place. So I began to explore the idea of place. I read books such as John Inge's influential *A Christian Theology of Place*, David Brown's *God and the Enchantment of Place* and Oliver O'Donovan's important article 'The Loss of a Sense of Place',[1] each of which seemed to resonate with where we were in our cultural moment and what I perceived to be a felt longing expressed by many for a sense of place identity and belonging. I found myself therefore in a strange position of now trying to question the arguments of those whom I found myself increasingly agreeing with. What motivated me, however, was that no matter how much I agreed with the premises of the arguments, I continued to disagree almost entirely with the conclusions.

Specifically, where I agreed with the instincts about place, and even with the historical importance of the parish structure, I could not see how these convictions should lead one to reject new forms of church out of hand. To make sense of all this I began reading about place beyond the theological literature, reaching out beyond the immediate debate and finding out about place in human geography. It was here that I discovered place to be a more complex category than many of the critics of the new churches presented it to be. Put simply, if place in the theology was fairly 'flat', mainly focused on boundaries and the static, place in the disciplines outside theology was dynamic and eventful. This understanding of place as dynamic – what I call in this book 'bounded and open' – made a lot of sense of what I was experiencing in the four churches. For what I learned most from these four churches – both parish and non – was that being present is not a simple thing. I saw how these churches had to work to become present to the places that they loved. I thus found in my research just how complex a task being present in place is for both the parish churches and the new churches, and simultaneously how little purchase the fact of being a parish church or not seemed to have on the church's imaginary and its ministry.

I loved my time with a parish church in a rural village, which was working out why it was that the church and village had somehow grown apart. In this location, the parish and place overlapped on a map perfectly. The village boundaries were the parish boundaries, and vice versa. The problem wasn't a geographical one, it was simply that the church – physically central – had somehow ceased to be vital. One of the fresh expressions I spent time with had recently shifted, from being spread over a region-wide geographical area, to now being rooted in one housing estate on the edge of town. They had been, if you like, pulled toward place out of love. Another parish church was deeply involved in its locale and had worked hard to make this a possibility. The interesting feature of this church was that it stood out from other churches around it in how well it loved its place. The neighbouring parishes shared the same challenges but had seen only decline and an increasing lack of community engagement. The final church I spent time with was a church we would now call a plant rather than a fresh expression, and it was the most divorced from place of the four. It certainly existed outside the parish structure. And yet I found here a hunger for place. Though the school hall they met in was incidental, there were many within the congregation who wanted to make more of the immediate locale, naming the obvious issues connected with pitching up week by week and not engaging with the streets and neighbourhoods around. From the front, the leaders of the church would speak a great deal of their love for the city; how they were called to be engaged in all areas of the city's life.

Thus is the complex picture when we consider how the Church of England churches are present to their places today. One theme that emerged strongly in the research was precisely this theme of love of place. It seemed to me that it was this love that motivated and made possible parish-like ministry, more than the other way round. That is, these churches found ways to love their places, feeling connected to them, irrespective of the structures. It was this love of place that became a focus. I felt strongly – and still do – that where the defences of the parish are right is in their commitment to this love, and where they are wrong is in trying to retain that love within the current structures. All of this is hard, because in one sense those structures have sustained the love that is sought. The parish has been the given form of the church's commitment to the life of the nation. So the answer as I saw it, was not to jump ship. Rather it was to question and to reimagine, to wrestle. Not then a choice between structures or none, inherited churches or not. Rather the challenge was and is to find structures that allow that love to take root. It is to receive what we have been gifted from our traditions, fanning into flame the love that they promised to maintain. So wrestle with the parish we must, and it is in the wrestling that the blessing is found. In this book I want to ask some of the questions I think we should be asking of the parish as it is practised today. Specifically, I want to think about what presence in place really means. Given the nature of place, and the nature of human person, we would do well to disassociate the parish *vocation* from the parish structure, even if just to give us enough imaginative space to think critically and hopefully.

In each of these tasks I see myself as just about holding on to the coat-tails of Andrew Rumsey's brilliant book, *Parish: A Christian Theology of Place*.[2] Rumsey's book is important because he is fully conscious of the criticism that the parish, 'easily becomes just a code word for "mere communitarian nostalgia"'. He is thus careful to avoid the temptation to defend the parish out of a mere regressivism, a hungering for the past and a failure to recognize its contemporary offering. Ultimately Rumsey does this through a rigorous theology in which he shows that place is both theologically vital and relative. *We are faithful not to place but to God, who shows himself to us in place.* All of this allows Rumsey to offer a more honest account of place and the parish; to see parish as central, without feeling bound to defend its form; to show how parish is a problematic category as much as it is a hopeful one.

Indeed, Rumsey at the end of his book is alive to what is one of the core observations of this one: that in secular geography theory, place is seen as a dynamic and complex reality.[3] What I am doing above all in this book then is taking up Rumsey's call for what he calls an 'evangelical appreciation for place', the groundwork for which he lays so well.[4] *Appreciation* for place because evangelicals like myself have tended to think in overly instrumental ways. But *evangelical* because presence in place must be about mission and action; the intentional bringing the things of God close to where his beloved creatures are.

My hope is that you read this book aware of where you are. This in two senses. First, that you read it aware of your current place, because the best way of thinking about place is to think about your own. Where is it that you currently are? Where do you feel you belong? Second, I hope you read from where you are in relation to the conversations about the parish. It might be that these conversations are very present to you, either because you have caught up with the latest Twitter spat or article on Unherd, or because they are your lived reality. The conversation may matter because you are trying to make sense of the parish in your own context. You may believe the parish needs saving, you may believe that such a cause is a distraction from everything else that really matters. Wherever you are reading from, my hope is that this book gives you some language and concepts to help make sense of the discussion. If there has been one guiding motivation for me in writing this book it is this: that it might help to improve the quality of the conversation.

Notes

1 John Inge, 2003, *A Christian Theology of Place*, Aldershot: Ashgate; David Brown, 2004, *God and the Enchantment of Place*, Oxford: Oxford University Press; Oliver O'Donovan, 2004, 'The Loss of a Sense of Place', in Oliver O'Donovan and Joan Lockwood O'Donovan, *Bonds of Imperfection: Christian Politics, Past and Present*, Grand Rapids, MI: Wm. B. Eerdmans, pp. 296–320. See also Philip Sheldrake, 2001, *Spaces for the Sacred: Place, Memory and Identity*, Baltimore,

MD: Johns Hopkins University Press; Timothy J. Gorringe, 2002, *A Theology of the Built Environment*, Cambridge: Cambridge University Press. For an overview of some of these approaches, see Sigurd Bergmann, 'Theology in its Spatial Turn', *Religion Compass*, 1:3 (2007), pp. 353–79.

2 Andrew Rumsey, 2017, *Parish: An Anglican Theology of Place*, London: SCM Press.

3 Rumsey, *Parish*, p. 187.

4 Rumsey, *Parish*, p. 170.

Introduction

While from the world's viewpoint, the Church of England's institutional influence has long been shrinking like a balloon, this slow puncture has not, by contrast, shrunk the Church's own view of its worldly reach and responsibility. National allegiance to the Church may be in freefall, but the Church's allegiance to the Nation remains as lofty as ever. In this, the Church is not so much clinging to the myth of its own significance as to that of the places it exists to serve.[1]

The Church of England and place are the themes of this book. Neither the church, nor place, is anything new. Yet in both instances something is up. Take place first. Place is the ground upon which all life has played out, and yet it is only in recent times that it has been observed as an idea; something we don't simply live in, but talk about. Our immediate past in the West has demonstrated the importance of the concept of place. Following the election of Donald Trump in the USA, and the Brexit referendum in the UK, there were many commentators who sought to make sense of what happened using the categories of place and space. We were witnessing, so it was suggested, the reassertion of place and locality: an event that was shocking only to the extent that we (or, at least, the commentariat) underestimated place's pervasive power on communities. Such a conclusion is not comprehensive, but it holds truth. In his book, *The Road to Somewhere*, David Goodhart argues that our political conversation today is marked by the clash of different understandings of place, between those whom he labels 'Anywheres' and 'Somewheres' respectively.[2] The latter,

Goodhart argues, define their identity in some sense according to their place: it matters that they are from a somewhere, that they are *of* a particular place. In contrast, for those Anywheres – generally university educated, mobile, travelled – identity is manufactured from materials other than geography. An Anywhere really is a global citizen, sharing more in common with an Anywhere from the other side of the globe than with a Somewhere who lives a few miles up the road. In this analysis, what so many people missed in the lead-up to the 2016 EU referendum in the UK, and the US Presidential Election across the water, was precisely this affective pull of place and the importance to so many Somewheres of their place, from their local neighbourhood through to their nation. Any perceived erosion of these places then, through immigration, or economic shifts, or change in cultural imaginary, was accordingly experienced as distress. Might it be that for many, the promise of a globalized world, in which every place becomes a part of a whole, is not received as gift but as threat?

The recent experience of a global pandemic has breathed further life into the conversations about place: a global event, shared by all and yet experienced at the most immediate level. We were quite literally rooted in our place. Consequently, each of us suddenly had to wrestle with the realities of rootedness. Would we flourish here or would we suffocate? Did the place we were destined to be in bring us to life or did it steal, kill and destroy? Many began to appreciate their immediate locales in new ways. For some, a sort of new local engagement followed the pandemic. Others were able to hold a tension of longings: it was good to be rooted for a time, but it was good to be free to leave. For some, the rootedness highlighted what they perhaps knew but had avoided up to that juncture: that this place was not for them. Place wasn't so much the issue; it was *this* place. And in the midst of it all we were made acutely aware of those for whom all the existential thinking about place was pure luxury. The lockdowns served to push many yet deeper into a place experienced as a cage. Rootedness for so many was not a gift but a horror.

And what of the second theme – the Church of England? In our time, the church finds itself dealing with acute challenges. I am always wary of speaking of a 'unique moment' in this regard: the challenges we face are never wholly unique – there is nothing new under the sun – and 'moments' can imply a singularity, when our challenges are multi-generational and historical. However, if there are particular challenges that we face then they concern the possibility of being a national church amid an ever-widening gap between church and nation, the parishes and their people; what Jeremy Morris describes as the 'growing dissonance' between the church and society.[3] Or, to put it differently and begin to make the connection between the two central themes of this book, we might say that the church is struggling to be fully rooted in the place that is England. At its best the parish is, in Jessica Martin's words, 'the kingdom leaven in the bread dough of its locality'.[4] The ground, how-ever, is shifting beneath our feet, and though the vision to be 'a Christian presence in every community' remains, the reality frequently fails to match it.

There is a pervading sense in our parishes, and has been for some time, that something is awry. A sense, perhaps, backed up by numbers: declining church attendance, declining occasional offices, declining stipendiary posts, declining just about every-thing. The numbers, though, only tell so much.[5] What I think has mattered far more are people's experiences: an incongru-ence between what was once known and the way things seem to be now. It is not my job here to wade into what is commonly known as the secularization debate, only to say that I take it for granted that we are living through a time we can rightly call 'post-Christendom'. From where we stand as an established church, the term refers to the ever-increasing possibility for most people to live their lives and mark the significant moments within them without recourse to the church.

What I reach for when discussing this with my students is not so much the numbers as the pictures. If you go into most parish vestries in the country you will find there some old photo albums, many of which were created as commemorations for significant birthdays in that church's life. And what always strikes me about these photos is the number of people in them. They are helpful pictures because they are not of Sunday worship. These are photos of crowds of people at summer fetes, harvest festivals, Whit walks, church days away to the beach. There are often pictures of Sunday school activities: I've seen many photos of a (male) vicar standing outside a church with literally hundreds of children standing around him. For me it is this that marks the change. The shift from the time captured in such pictures to where we are now. For the clergy in the pictures, 'being present to the people of the parish' was a very different task to the one we ask of our ministers today. The church in so many places (not every place, as we shall see) was simply assumed to be important; it was a part of many people's imaginary, even if not their immediacy. Run a Sunday school at 3 p.m. every Sunday afternoon and children would come. Organize an outing to the beach and people would sign up. In other words, in many places the church was present *simply by being the church in that place*. Again, I do not want to romanticize this. All the evidence demonstrates just how complicated the history is and how much variety there was across the nation.[6] My point, however, is not that the church was 'once in health and now is not'. It is rather that within the last several generations (at least since the Second World War) we have witnessed a significant shift in how the local parish churches sit within their parishes, so that someone who is in their fifties or sixties, and has been in church for most of their life, will be able to recognize a substantive difference in the way that the church and the place interact. This seems to me simply the common experience of most long-time congregants in our parishes.

In response to all this, the church has sought to effect change. I am most interested here in the shift that has occurred in the lead-up to, and following, the publication of the church report *Mission-shaped Church*.[7] In the long history of the Church of England, no report has been as widely read and very few have had as rapid an impact. Following the 1994 report *Breaking*

4

New Ground, which attempted to find a place within the Church of England for the growing number of church plants and house churches, *Mission-shaped Church* paved the way for a number of pieces of legislation that gave official status to these new projects, which then tended to be grouped together as 'Fresh Expressions' of church.[8] Through Bishops' Mission Orders (BMOs), bishops were given authority to ordain pioneer ministers and establish new churches, many of which work outside existing parish structures. Martyn Percy's response to *Mission-shaped Church*, that 'never before has [the Church of England] sought to legalize a move outside the traditional parish system'[9] is, of course, overstated. The Church of England has always consisted of more than the (geographical) parish, the place of chaplaincy being just one example. However, he is right to claim there is something new going on: formal and legal recognition of non-parochial *churches* – of Church of England churches that relate to the world other than through a geographically designated area. It's no exaggeration to say that these developments mark a new chapter in the story of the Church of England as the national church.

In the 20 years since *Mission-shaped Church* was published the church has seen a huge increase in activity to start new churches. Data from the Church Growth programme published in 2013 suggested that fresh expressions were the cause of numerical growth in many dioceses, and by this stage made up 10 per cent of all church attendance, equating to one new average-sized diocese.[10] Across 21 of the Church's dioceses, there had been over 11,000 fresh expressions started – stretching back to 1992, but a majority following *Mission-shaped Church*. Since 2014, some 1,600 new worshipping communities have been planted or grafted across 31 dioceses,[11] and since 2017 the church has invested over £140 million of its assets in new missional projects, many of which involve the establishing of new worshipping communities.[12] In June 2018, the House of Bishops agreed that planting new churches can 'become(s) a normal part of a diocese's approach to mission'[13] and a majority of dioceses now have a target for the numbers of new churches they aim to see started in the next five or ten years. As part of its vision for the 2020s, the national church announced plans to establish 10,000 new lay- and ordained-led churches, which was in addition to the 10,000 target announced by the recently established Gregory Centre for Church Multiplication led by a Bishop for Church Planting – what it called the Myriad project.[14]

The response to all of this has been mixed to say the least. In the first chapter of this book, I shall outline some of the early theological critiques levelled against what was perceived to be the theological (and thus ecclesiological) deficiencies of *Mission-shaped Church*, the arguments that proved to be fairly paradigmatic for all that followed. At the centre of it all was a focus on the parish; the only ecclesial form, so it was argued, with the historical and theological credibility to allow us to make sense of the challenges facing the church today. In recent years these concerns have found a uniting voice in the Save the Parish movement, with its published manifesto, events and growing list of supporters, all of which has drawn interest not only within the church – the high frequency of coverage in the *Church Times* – but also from the national press.[15] Writing of the movement, Revd Marcus Walker offered a rallying call to stand in the then-upcoming General Synod elections:

> So, stand … Stand if you want to save the parish, because these are your parishes and this is the only important question for the next five years. Stand because this might really be the last chance to save the church we love.[16]

The parish matters as the locus where the two themes of this book, place and the church, converge. When we ask the 'where' question of the Church of England, we very quickly must turn to the language of parish. The parish is more than a structure or organizational principle; it is the very imaginary of the Church of England. When I was ordained, I was ordained not to a church, but to a parish: committed therefore not simply to a congregation but to all the people of this place. We are used to thinking 'top-down' in our age, but if you think about the church from the bottom up, you see that the parish is the basic unit of the church's ministry – parishes organized into deaneries, in turn into dioceses. So what are we to make of the realities faced in the parishes today? If the connection between the churches and their places wanes it should force us to ask some very searching questions. For on what other basis do we think we really can be the Church of England? If the churches lose connection with parishes, then the church has lost its connection with the nation.

The polarization of the debate

This book is as much about the debate about the parish as it is about the parish itself. Specifically, it is an attempt to move us beyond the intransigence that is so often its character. If polarization has become a feature of our political discourse, I suggest that it is no less prevalent here. 'Are you for the parish, or for this newer stuff?' I sometimes get asked. And that underlying assumption rears its head all the time: 'Should we be pouring all this money into new things, or should we just focus on what we've got?' 'The parish is dead; we need to start again.' 'Church planting is a denial of the parish.' This book is about why I think this type of conversation is fundamentally, and deeply, *unwise*.

The process of polarization does two interrelated things, which always work against wisdom. We become more con-vinced of our own perspective, and we become increasingly incapable of recognizing the perspectives of others. We thus end up caught in a vicious circle: the more entrenched we become, the less we hear, and the less we hear, the less we self-critique and learn, thereby closing ourselves off yet further. Eventually, we find ourselves in a position where we assume that to hold to a certain conviction must, therefore, necessarily look like rejecting another. As if there were no other way to hold our conviction than to be against 'them'. This is the danger with, for example, being 'for the parish' or 'for church planting'. Set up like this, the assumption becomes ingrained so that to be 'for the parish', I must therefore be against church planting. But this cannot be right, for a whole host of reasons, and not least because every parish church must have at some point been started (planted). Thus, to be 'for the parish' cannot mean to be 'against church planting' in principle, any more than to be for the threefold order of ministry means to be against lay leadership. But so too vice versa: I know many who are engaged in church planting who – because of the cultural stream they have been swimming in – have not stopped to ask the value of parish churches. In other words, they have imbibed a certain assumption that inherited parish churches are probably a cause of decline.

Polarization thus leads to a perpetuating of givens. We tend towards doing what we've always done, only now we feel more justified in doing it. But what if? What if, say, there was something brilliant about church planting, but *this* plant is being done not very well? What if instead of this church plant being open for all, rooted in its local community, and seeking to work in partnership with other local churches, it is instead parasitic on its community, in animosity with other churches, and interested only in its own membership? But equally the question must be asked in the other direction. What if there is genuinely something brilliant about the parish model, but *this* parish church is doing the parish badly? What if instead of the parish church being open to all, rooted in its local community, and seeking to work in partnership with other local churches, it is instead insular and exclusive, interested only in its own survival, and generally inhospitable to visitors?

In these examples I have stated things in the negative. Fundamentally, however, polarization stops us seeing what *could* be, it stops us receiving good insight from others. Think, for example, of the ordinand who comes into training with their 'for the parish' stall clearly set out, but who receives from the church planter the apostolic zeal and entrepreneurial insight to connect with the 90 per cent in the parish who currently have zero connection with the church; the skills to start something from scratch; the confidence to ask whether there might be a new place where the church might be formed. And likewise the church planter who receives from the inherited parish church the value of faithful, long-term commitment to place, of being invested in local secular institutions, and the privilege afforded by being the Church of England to be welcomed into the most significant and intimate moments of people's lives.

The system theorist Edwin Friedman argues in his book, *A Failure of Nerve*, that one of the features of what he calls a chronically anxious or 'imaginatively gridlocked' system is either-or, black-and-white thinking. He argues that 'such intense polarizations [are] always symptomatic of underlying emotional processes rather than of the subject matter of the polarizing issue.'[17] My sense is that this is a fairly apt description of the conversation around the parish and indeed of many issues the church faces. There has been much anxiety-driven thinking within the Church of England. Anxiety that has worked itself out, therefore, both in a tendency to grasp more tightly to received traditions and practices, or the opposite, to jettison these in search of the new. This book attempts to move beyond such polarities to something more fruitful. My claim is that the parish vocation is something precious, worth holding on to. And yet it is imperative that we find ways of differentiating the vocation from the structure that, up until now, has been the given form it has taken. If we do this, then we might be able to reimagine the parish for our time. The premise of the cure of souls wanes as the connection between parishes and their places wanes. If the premise continues to hold weight into the future then it will be because we manage to establish churches that are present to their place.

The Church of England and place are the themes of this book, but my thinking is shaped by two concepts: tradition and instinct. Before I proceed, it is worth outlining why I see them as foundational.

Tradition

In his book, *After Virtue*, the philosopher Alasdair MacIntyre says this about traditions:

> When a tradition is in good order it is always partially constituted by an argument about the goods the pursuit of which gives to that tradition its particular point and purpose ... Traditions, when vital, embody continuities of conflict.[18]

For MacIntyre, a tradition, if it is really to matter, must be an ongoing debate, what he calls, 'continuities of conflict'. We should be continually asking: What is this tradition, and what is it for (what 'goods' was it intended to bring about)? MacIntyre is saying that when it comes to traditions we must avoid two extremes. On the one hand, the temptation is simply to accept traditions as they are, as if they were set in stone. The other danger is just as prevalent, however: that we too easily jettison them. 'That was then, this is now. We don't need to do things like that anymore ...'

My suggestion is that we should think of the parish structure as a tradition that we have received. It is the way things have been done, and the pattern of life that we find ourselves within. In this sense, as a tradition, we must wrestle with the parish structure. But if MacIntyre is right, then what matters is the *way* we wrestle with it. Not to place ourselves as either 'rejecting' or 'accepting' it. The challenge is to debate it, question and reimagine it. Uncritical acceptance and sheer rejection are signs of lazy thinking. If we put it in the terms of the conversation at hand, we might ask the question MacIntyre calls us to thus: What were the goods that the parish structure aimed to bring about, and how are those goods to be pursued today?

This then is my basic argument. The parish is credible, but it needs reimagining if we are to be faithful to its intention – to its 'goods'. In this sense I am convinced that there is something worth fighting for in what Karl Rahner called the parochial principle.[19] The Church of England has no monopoly on such a principle. Rahner himself is speaking of the Roman Catholic churches, and the parish structure, as Jeremy Morris points out, is a feature of European Christendom.[20] By parish principle, I mean not so much the structure, as this sense of the Church of England's unique vocation. This vocation of the parish is ultimately about an interplay between the centre and the local. At the centre the church wields influence: soft, and limited legislative, powers. There are bishops in the House of Lords, and the church continues to serve as a holder for some of the most significant moments in the nation's life. The church can only be at the centre, however, by being present in the local, in every place. Thus, the church's connection to the life of the nation is parochial in form: it is to their parish church that every person has a claim, and from here that baptism, marriage and rites of death are offered. There is a unique ecclesiology, which is both a result and sustainer of the parish. It is an ecclesiology in which the church is implicated in the life of the nation. I mean by this that the Church of England has deemed itself to be not apart from the nation – in a simple church–world distinction – but somehow within the nation. Carrying her pains, celebrating her joys. And all of this is possible because of that imagined local commitment. Integrated in place, there and present.

Another way of getting at this is through the language of responsibility: the church has been given a responsibility for the cure of souls for every person in the nation. It is a strange vocation, and one that is historically particular (you couldn't quite make it up). It is a vocation we trust as God-given, breathed by the Spirit, even as it is delivered to us through the state. It is not the vocation of every denomination in the nation and certainly not of every church in our world (including those in the rest of the Anglican Communion), or through history. I take it to be neutral in terms of its benefits and pitfalls; no better or worse than any other. And it is ultimately precarious, reliant not simply on the church's self-definition, but on the nation's entrusting to it. In this sense it is a gift rather than something owned. The parish structure as we have it has existed at least since the system was settled by the end of the Middle Ages, and the vocation transcends this, reaching back to the first entrusting of the gospel and its church as the basis of our communal life. But there is no guarantee that it will be thus for ever. The Lord gives and the Lord takes away. To paraphrase Paul, we are to work out this vocation with fear and trembling. If there are accusations of arrogance to be levelled against the church in this regard, then they will come (and should come!) when the church mistakes this gift for possession.

My claim is that for as long as the gift is given it must be received well. This then is the task of recognizing, assessing and reimagining the parish in our time. Taking seriously the gift of the vocation to presence and working out how we do this in our place and places. In this sense, the 'goods' of which MacIntyre speaks concern the vocation to presence in place, the cure of souls. And once we name that, we are able to ask the vital question: How then do we achieve or protect those goods today, in our time? My argument is that the goods assumed to inhere within the parish structure are different from the structure itself. And it is in holding those apart that we can begin to imagine the ways in which the vocation to presence may be rethought for today. Again, the likely answer of such an investigation is that the structure does some things well and others not so well. MacIntyre, I think, assumes that when it comes to traditions, it is likely that the tradition is very far from perfect, and it is likely that the tradition is very far from diabolical.

Instincts

The second underlying category is instinct. Instincts are something that I find myself repeatedly talking to my students about. 'That's a good critique of her position', I will say. 'But what are the instincts that lie beneath it? Why is she making that point?' I think it is vital if we are to dialogue well as Christians that we should understand what I have called one another's *theological instincts.* When the debate becomes polarized, it is these instincts that we tend to miss.

Mostly, we use instinct to refer to a physical response: it is instinct that causes us to drop a match as the flame moves too quickly towards our finger, for example. However, I want to suggest that it is also appropriate to use instinct in reference to our mental responses; to what we say or write and, indeed, to what we think. Beneath our expressed responses lie a host of instincts that cause us to respond as we do. This is of course not a new claim, nor an especially profound one. It is one of the accepted mantras of our own twenty-first-century world view that we each speak from a host of convictions and experiences; that we each have 'lenses' through which we see the world, and from which we then respond. This is what I mean by instinct: on the basis of these lenses, we *want* to respond in a particular way – even before we've had the chance to think about it. It is this conviction that lies behind 'unconscious bias' training, which has become a central part of most training pathways for businesses and institutions. What underpins such training is the conviction that we will each have instincts that mean we will respond in certain ways, and that these instincts may well be subterranean; unknown to us, just as their consequences may, likewise, go unseen. Unconscious bias training thus simply picks up on a truth that we have determined to be a good one: that maturity entails becoming increasingly aware of the patterns of thought and experiences that cause us to respond in the ways that we do. The more self-aware we can each become, the more chance we will have of being able to receive the other rather than simply reacting.

The challenge for each of us, therefore, and not least those of us who claim to belong to Christ, is to become aware of our instincts. Indeed, we might say that this is one image of what it means to be increasingly conformed to the image of Christ, what we can call discipleship: from Jesus' comedic image of the person who is so busy picking out specks that he misses the plank, to the Pauline themes of transformation of the mind and the new behavioural responses that should flow out of being grasped again by the truth of the gospel.[21] So much of the New Testament seems to be about the difficult task of observing, naming and then transforming (or, better, allowing the transformation) of what lies beneath. Noticing the externals, but digging into the internals. Into the instincts. In this sense, my use of the example of unconscious bias training might be in danger of taking us down an unhelpful path. For although this type of training focuses on instincts that are negative (or, at least, that lead to dehumanizing behaviours), it is clearly not the case that all our instincts are bad. In fact, as so much recent theological writing reminds us, the goal of our discipleship is not so much to lose our instincts as to develop new ones; instincts that are more in tune with the truth of God.[22] We are to become the sort of people who *instinctually* think, speak and behave in ways that are faithful to the gospel. We get it wrong of course; this side of the New Creation our instincts will inevitably be mixed, and we will not always speak, think and behave from instincts that are shaped by the love of God. But the call remains: to develop gospel-shaped instincts.

So far, so good. The problem, however, is that the gospel is not monochrome. If it were, we might expect Christians to be working towards shared instinctual responses; Christians who all respond in the same way. But the gospel is multifaceted and is made up of a number of different emphases that cohere within one reality. We see this when we read the Gospels. The same Jesus who tells us to hate 'father and mother, wife and children, brothers and sisters' (Luke 14.26) is the same Jesus who amid agony seeks the well-being and protection of his own mother (John 19.26–27). The point is that these are not contradictory, but are different emphases within the same reality of the Kingdom. Both are instincts. The instinct to care for family is good. The instinct to deny everything for the sake of the Kingdom is good. On the flip side, self-denial might indeed look very much like care for one's mother, but care for one's own family might well be the manifestation of a sort of tribalism, rooted in fear and pride. In this way, the New Testament takes instincts seriously and, when it assesses human character, it is just as, if not more, interested in why we do, as in what we do.

I remember first becoming interested in the idea of theological instincts when I read the missiologist Lesslie Newbigin's little book on the church, *The Household of God*.[23] In this book, Newbigin presents what he sees as the three ways in which the Christian church has understood what it means to participate in the body of Christ; that is, to *be* the church. These he calls the 'Protestant', the 'Catholic' and the 'Pentecostal'. It is not my purpose here to unpack each of these, but only to point out that when I first read Newbigin's book I remember being amazed by the way in which these three 'ways' seemed to make sense of everything I had been reading about ecclesiology up to that point. Newbigin had put language around the diversity of theological approaches to the church that I had found so much life in, from Catholic writers to modern missiologists like Melba Padilla Maggay, or Newbigin himself. And Newbigin's central point of course is that *all three ways are faithful to the gospel*. The Protestant, with its emphasis on the Word of God that constantly comes to us from 'outside'; the Catholic, with its deep conviction that God is concerned with *this* world, and that historical continuity with the events of the Gospels matters; and the Pentecostal, with its awareness that it is the Holy Spirit who forms the church and that God really is present, in our midst, here and now. Each of these is true to the gospel. Each is, in that sense, 'right'. I remember being fascinated by what sort of church you would end up with if you over- or underemphasized one or the other (Newbigin does a masterly job of outlining the various consequences of dropping one or two for the sake of a dominant one). Nowhere does Newbigin refer to these three as instincts, but I want to suggest that this is precisely what they are. They are three different, gospel-shaped, faithful *instincts*. And they are, like all instincts, formed through experience, preference, habit and everything else, until they become a part of who we are. So when we are faced with a discussion about ecclesiology – for example, the parish structure – something like Newbigin's book gives us a framework to help understand why it might be that we disagree as we do. The question we need to get to quickly, beneath the presenting issue, is: What are the theological instincts that they hold which mean that they see things differently to me? In fact, before asking that question, the first question must surely be: What are my own theological instincts that mean *I* see things the way *I* do?

I want to suggest that the parish is an issue, like many others, that reveals some of these theological instincts. Wherever one is on the imagined spectrum of responses to the parish structure – from staunch defender, through sympathetic critic, to fierce opponent – we sit where we do in part because of theological instincts. And it is these theological instincts that require our attention. This is a book about these instincts, and about what is going on in the polarity of the debate around the parish. What are the instincts of those who value the parish, and how might these instincts play out in practice? But to return to my earlier language, I hope this book will help us to mature in those instincts. I hope to be able to demonstrate what it might look like for the church to act wisely out of the theological instincts that are ours together in this body.

I said earlier that the parish vocation is a strange and precarious gift; one that comes from outside the church rather than as something it dreams up for itself. This 'strangeness' of the vocation to presence is an important corrective to the inevitable tendencies towards ecclesial arrogance of which the church is often accused. The vocation does not belong to the church as possession. I am convinced, however, that as well as being a strange gift, the parish vocation does resonate today, both inside and outside the church. That is, it makes sense of our cultural moment and, in particular, of many theological and cultural instincts around place. In this sense the commitment to the parish is not quite as odd as it may have felt in certain circles even 20 years ago. It seems somehow appropriate for a church today to be asking how it might be more rooted, more present, less 'manufactured' and more implicated in the reality of people's lives and communities.

In Chapter 1, I explore the early criticisms of *Mission-shaped Church* and the resulting Fresh Expressions movement, observing how these play out into the contemporary discussions about the parish. The argument I make is that beneath the presenting issues the instincts at play concern place. What these 'defenders of the parish' articulate, therefore, is a deep longing for place – what I call an 'affective pull' towards place. I show why I think this affective pull is a good thing, and one that we need to take seriously in our ecclesiology. Chapter 2 takes up the theme of the debate itself. I seek to show how we might better disagree with one another and what it might mean to take forward MacIntyre's conviction that fidelity to tradition looks like debate rather than uncritical appropriation or rejection. I try to give this a Church of England flavour by showing why disagreement over practices and structure is written into the heart of the Church of England's identity. My claim is that the affective pull towards place may in fact lead us to critique the parish structures more than affirm them. In Chapter 3, I pick up the theme of place. If the church is to be present in place then it matters what we believe place actually is. I show why place is a more complicated reality than many of the defenders of the parish assume it to be. Place is what I call 'bounded openness': consistent and definable, but always changing and formed in a relationship of places. In the final chapter, I argue that this understanding of place demands that our pursuit of presence be about more than simply coverage or proximity. It is an attempt to show what it might look like to have presence in place as a guiding value in our ecclesiology. My claim is that this will necessitate new churches as well as inherited ones. It is questionable whether the church's preferred language of 'mixed ecology' is the best terminology to use, but the premise at least carries weight: if the church is to become present and make vital the parish commitment, then we should expect to see an array of churches and expressions, drawn by the Spirit of God into real places.

Notes

1 Andrew Rumsey, 2017, *Parish: An Anglican Theology of Place*, London: SCM Press, pp. 112–13.

2 David Goodhart, 2017, *The Road to Somewhere: The New Tribes Shaping British Politics*, London: Penguin Random House.

3 Jeremy Morris, 2022, *A People's Church: A History of the Church of England*, London: Profile, p. 380.

4 Jessica Martin, 2016, 'Introduction', in Jessica Martin and Sarah Coakley (eds), *For God's Sake: Re-Imagining Priesthood and Prayer in a Changing Church*, London: Canterbury Press.

5 As many have pointed out, the numbers are a blunt instrument when it comes to this complex issue. Not only does the process of 'decline' look and feel very different across different parts of the country, but for a church that seeks to be for all people and especially its non-attendees, it is always a challenge to know how to make sense of Sunday attendance figures. The better measure I think is that of the number of baptisms, weddings and funerals taking place in church, which have seen significant decline over a long period. These matter because they are an indication of the connection between church and nation, not in *our* mind, but in the mind of the nation. For a church that seeks to be for all, these numbers indicate a problem.

6 It is not uncommon, for example, to hear people who tend to question the 'supposed decline' in the Church of England refer to the Bishop of London's lament on Easter Sunday in 1800 that only six people received communion at St Paul's Cathedral; the point being that there have always been times and places where the Church of England has struggled. Even the pushback, however, is complicated. To be sure, the Bishop of London did say that, but on that same day there were 311 communicants at St Mary's Kilkenny; a trend seen in many other local parish returns.

7 Archbishops' Council, 2004, *Mission-shaped Church: Church Planting and Fresh Expressions of Church in a Changing Context*, London: Church House Publishing.

8 *A Measure for Measures* was produced in 2004 – almost simultaneously with *MSC* – with the focus of assessing the various measures passed by the Church of England in the previous 30 or so years that had sought to provide greater flexibility in the church's ecclesial structures. The recommendations in *A Measure for Measure* would lead to a new Pastoral Measure in 2005 and, in 2007, to a reforming of the 1983 Pastoral Measure to create one new Measure. See Archbishops' Council, 2004, *A Measure for Measures in Mission and Ministry: Report of the Review of the Dioceses, Pastoral and Related Measures*, London: Church House Publishing.

9 Martyn Percy, 2008, 'Introduction', in *Evaluating Fresh Expressions: Explorations in Emerging Church*, Louise Nelstrop and Martyn Percy (eds), Norwich: Canterbury Press, p. xxi.

10 See Church Growth Research Project; Report on Strand 3b: *An Analysis of Fresh Expressions of Church and Church Plants*, at www.churchofengland.org/sites/default/files/2019-06/church_growth_research_fresh_expressions_-_strand_3b_oct13_-_the_report.pdf, accessed 02.02.2022.

11 Strategic Investment Board Annual Report, 2018, at https://www.churchofengland.org/sites/default/files/2021-07/SIB%20annual%20report%202018.pdf, accessed 02.02.2022.

12 Triennium Funding Working Group, 2019, 'National Church Spending Plans for 2020–22', at https://www.churchofengland.org/sites/default/files/2019-06/Triennium%20Funding%20Working%20Group%20Figures%2021.06.pdf, accessed 02.02.2022.

13 House of Bishops, 2018, 'Church Planting and the Mission of the Church: Statement by the House of Bishops', at https://www.churchofengland.org/sites/default/files/2018-06/CHURCH%20PLANTING%20AND%20THE%20MISSION%20OF%20THE%20CHURCH%20-%20June%202018_0.pdf, accessed 10.10.2021.

14 Gregory Centre, Myriad Project, at https://ccx.org.uk/myriad/, accessed 02.06.2022. It is important to say that some of these new churches (it is impossible to say how many) are not additions to the parish, but are rather church grafts or 'revitalization' projects.

15 See Save the Parish, at https://savetheparish.com, accessed 02.06.2022. For the national press, see, for example, Harriet Sherwood, 2021, 'A Church Without Walls: Anglicanism Divided on Shift away from Tradition', *The Guardian*, 30 August; Emma Thompson, 2021, 'Parish churches are a "spiritual NHS"', *The Telegraph*, 24 December.

16 Marcus Walker, 2021, 'Is This the Last Chance to Save the Church of England?', *The Spectator*, 10 July.

17 Edwin Friedman, 2007, *A Failure of Nerve: Leadership in the Age of the Quick Fix*, New York: Church Publishing.

18 MacIntyre's account of tradition can be found in Alasdair MacIntyre, 1985, *After Virtue*, 2nd edn, London: Duckworth, pp. 204–25.

19 Karl Rahner, 1963, *Theological Investigations II*, London: Darton, Longman & Todd, pp. 283–318.

20 Morris writes: 'Some Anglicans like to parade the myth that the parish system is the heart of the Church of England and that it represents a distinct, almost uniquely Anglican concept of pastoral ministry. But there is nothing distinctively Anglican about the parish.' Jeremy Morris, *People's Church*, p. 14. It is interesting to note that the Pentecostal denomination The Redeemed Christian Church of God (RCCG) uses the language of 'parish' and are making progress in their vision

to see such parishes formed five minutes' walking distance from every town in the country.

21 Paul does this repeatedly. A classic example is in Colossians 3.13 (cf. Ephesians 4.32): 'Bear with one another and, if anyone has a complaint against another, forgive each other; just as the Lord has forgiven you, so you also must forgive.' In other words, Paul is saying something like, 'Be more forgiving, but the key to this is not to try harder, but instead to dwell in the truth of your own forgiveness, that is (and in my terms) to develop a new set of instincts.' I see this as a frequent argument in Paul's letters, captured in his famous exhortation to the church in Rome in Romans 12.2.

22 This is too large a theme to try and reference here. One crucial thinker in this stream is Stanley Hauerwas, whose work I shall return to in the next chapter. As a good introduction to this idea for my students, I recommend Sam Wells, 2004, *Improvisation: The Drama of Christian Ethics*, London: SPCK, and James K. A. Smith, 2016, *You are What You Love*, Grand Rapids, MI: Brazos.

23 Lesslie Newbigin, 1964, *The Household of God: Lectures on the Nature of the Church*, London: SCM Press.

I

Longing for Place

They circle the area as they work out which direction to fly in
... no one really knows the true nature of the maps they con-
sult. Is it a feeling for them? A discomfort? A pull? I imagine
it is a kind of incompleteness, as though they've left part of
themselves behind. How home must tug at them.[1]

In this chapter, I want to explore the instincts of those who
have sought to defend the parish. My central conviction is that
there are good theological reasons to defend the parish structure against whatever is perceived to be working against it. I
shall begin by addressing the arguments of these 'defenders of
the parish' before moving on to explore the instincts at play.
What is clear is that when one begins to explore the work on
this area, the concept of 'place' quickly comes to the fore. This
term will therefore be the concern in the second part of this
chapter: place, and its close, yet idiosyncratic cousin, space.

The three responses I will explore have been around for
some time.[2] As argued in the Introduction they are, however,
paradigmatic of what has followed and articulate the essential
theological commitments of those suspicious of the ecclesiology written into and out of *Mission-shaped Church*. The
other thing to point out is that they are firm in the distinction
they establish between parish and non, inherited and new. This
distinction is not representative of everyone who might seek to
defend something of the parish. It is helpful for my purposes,
however: the stark distinction offers us a clear presentation of
the theological instincts at play.

The defenders of the parish

The first of the critiques is also the most substantial and I start with it since it does in large part cover the themes that shape the other two. *For the Parish*, by Andrew Davison and Alison Milbank is, in its own words, 'a thoroughgoing critique of fresh expressions on theological and philosophical grounds'.[3] I see in the book three core criticisms levelled at Fresh Expressions. The first is that the movement is founded on a philosophical mistake, namely the assertion that form can be divorced from content or, as they argue of Fresh Expressions, the 'kernel' of the gospel can be separated from its 'husk' of church form, practices and so on.[4] For Davison and Milbank, however, following Ludwig Wittgenstein, this separation is untenable. As they argue, the church *is* its form just as, for example, the meaning of a piece of art lies in its physicality.[5]

The second and third criticisms flow out of this initial per-ceived mistake. So, second, they see in this movement a tendency to do away with that which has gone before, in favour of that which is new. Fresh Expressions, they claim, values 'new over established', 'innovation over common worship', 'novelty over stability', the 'chosen over the given' and 'pastiche over authenticity'.[6] Third, once the church's essence is reduced to a series of beliefs or propositions and its *being* as an entity is accordingly seen as secondary, it becomes difficult to affirm the church *itself* as part of the goal of God's redemptive activ-ity. Fresh Expressions, they argue, make the church *functional*: it becomes a means to an end, rather than an end in itself.[7] Instead, they argue that salvation has an 'ecclesial dimension'; that is, it is imperative that church – in its outward forms – lives here and now what it will be in the age to come. And for them, since God's telos for the church is that it should be diverse rather than monochrome, so the church now must be 'mixed and harmonious in the face of difference and enmity'.[8] And it is at this point that the authors find Fresh Expressions most prob-lematic. They argue that in line with thinking from the 'Church growth movement' (what they describe as a 'market approach' to ecclesiology[9]), Fresh Expressions advocates the creation of churches that are targeted at a particular demographic so that they become established upon individual preference and like-minded individuals. Fresh Expressions then, they argue, encourages 'segregation', a tendency towards 'homogeneity' and thus serves to be a denial of the gospel of reconciliation.[10]

John Milbank, in his provocatively titled article, 'Stale Expressions: The Management- Shaped Church', shares a great deal with that of Davison and Milbank. In particular, he takes issue with the nature of Fresh Expressions as establishing church amid particular demographics. One section makes this point with force:

> [The] idea that the church should 'plant' itself in various sordid and airless interstices of our contemporary world, instead of calling people to 'come to church', is wrongheaded, because the refusal to come out of oneself and *go to* church is simply the refusal of church *per se*.[11]

The church, therefore, far from seeking to situate itself within existing 'networks' of relationship, must necessarily critique networks, given that this way of relating perpetuates a divided and siloed society; one in which we each relate only to those who appeal to us or are useful to us.

Martyn Percy, our final critic, raises many of the same concerns as the previous two. The critique of Fresh Expressions' perceived fascination with 'newness' is there, so too is the whole idea of 'targeted' or 'niche' church, which Percy, like the authors of *For the Parish*,[12] see originating in Donald McGavran's work on church growth theory.[13] Percy adds to these the possibility that fresh expressions are established more through a 'post-institutionalism' than genuine missional call: he observes Fresh Expressions as being a 'bourgeoisie phenomenon', formed around a 'thirty-forty-something age group beholden to "fresh" and "organic" concepts ...'.[14] Above all, though, Percy's strongest contribution to the critique of Fresh Expressions is his claim that such churches are fundamentally a denial of the call to impact, even to 'Christianize and convert society'.[15] As Percy sees it, because fresh expressions necessarily exist as attractional groups, gathered on the basis of individual choice, they work against the public and institutional nature of the church. In other words, they have abandoned the possibility of working for the common good. He summarizes: '[Fresh Expressions] legitimize the retreat from the duties (and occasional drudgery) of supporting and sustaining larger organisations that seek to offer something to society ... that sustain our social and spiritual capital.'[16]

The instincts of the parish

It might be that, from the brief overview of the critiques of Fresh Expressions above, some theological instincts have already become clear. The one I wish to highlight is what I call the theological instinct about the church's *difference*. What runs through each of the critiques I have selected is a wariness that the church might fail to be distinctively the church; looking and behaving like any other institution. Each writer is keen to stress that the church has been called to live according to the truths of the gospel, and thus that it should necessarily feel, look and act differently from the world around it.[17] The concerns levelled at the feet of *Mission-shaped Church* and Fresh Expressions can perhaps be summed up in Davison and Milbank's claim that 'sociology is allowed to triumph over theology'.[18] In other words, rather than seeking to understand and then establish the gospel-shaped form of the church (theology), the Fresh Expressions movement (and others like it) has sought first to understand the culture (sociology) and, for the sake of a missional impact, have shaped the church accordingly. In contrast, the writers agree that the gospel is a *reality* that includes the church, rather than a set of ideas that can take a variety of expressions. Thus, the church must take a particular form; it must look like a particular set of practices, ways of gathering and ministering.

Above all, each of these writers sees the church as called to be distinctive from what I will label here simply 'modernity'.[19] This moment – our culture, art, academia, politics, economics; in other words, every aspect of our existence – has certain features that are seen to be opposed to the truths held in the good news of Christ. It is these features we see identified in these critiques, be it post-institutionalism or networking. So the argument goes: the church is called to be countercultural, to be shaped by the story of the gospel, rather than the story of modernity. And all this so that it might tell of a truer story, to out-narrate the stories that modernity tells us about what it is to be human, to flourish and find meaning. In Davison and Milbank's words: 'We need communities that exemplify the character of the Church, strikingly themselves, in sharp contradistinction to the world ... a witness, a counter-culture and a refuge.'[20]

Again, the important thing is that we recognize the deep theological instinct at play here. Whether or not we agree with the way these critics outwork that instinct (and this book is an attempt to show that the instinct should not *necessarily* lead to the conclusions they reach), the fact is that the instinct itself is surely wise. Davison and Milbank's borrowed question does hit home: 'What would it profit the church to gain the whole world but to lose her own soul?'[21] The argument is that in her missionary task, not all options are open to the church. How else is the church to be missional besides being different? And underpinning this of course is virtually the whole of the New Testament's witness to what the church is. Not a tool through which God offers a message, but a foretaste of the age to come: a model of divine love (John 13); God's heirs (Romans 8); Christ's ambassadors, and the very righteousness of God (2 Corinthians 5); a royal priesthood (1 Peter); the list goes on and on.

And it is to the parish that these writers then turn as the holder for all this. The parish, they argue, is the church in her difference from the world. Thus, the parish structure sets the church in responsibility rather than self-interest; connection to the past rather than an obsession with the new; serving all within a geographical space rather than simply those it aims its mission towards; engagement within the messy realities of human life rather than the glossy and manufactured. In all of the defences of the parish that have followed these initial critiques, one can witness these same claims occurring again and again. The parish is the church in her difference from modernity. 'An antidote to secularity's pressures', writes Emma Thompson in *The Telegraph*.[22]

There is more that must be said. And it is at this point that the language of place comes in.

Place and space

The consensus among proponents of the parish is this: if there is one way in which the church is called to be distinctive from modernity, it is by *taking seriously the idea of place*. What I want to suggest is that this language of place becomes a sort of holder for all the concerns about new churches and for all the perceived goods of the parish structure. Thus, if a symptom of modernity's ills is a deep sense of placelessness, then the church stands apart by affirming place in all its messiness, complexity and limit. This argument has been set out convincingly elsewhere, and it is not my desire to reproduce those pieces by giving a comprehensive account here.[23] However, a brief summary will be helpful.

I begin by making a contrast between two terms: space and place. The terms themselves have significant linguistic roots,[24] but at this point it will be it enough to recognize that whereas space refers to physicality and measurability, place is a richer concept.[25] One of the most helpful ways I have come across to explain this difference is that of 'house' and 'home'. A house is space: it describes the physical area that someone lives in. 'Home', however, is a fuller description. You can portray a house to someone by sending them some pictures or giving them the dimensions or showing them the colour of the walls.

But to describe your home is a more complicated task. To do so would certainly involve a physical description, but would quite quickly need to draw in more. Giving an account of one's home is more a poetic than a scientific task. In this sense, space is a neutral category: it has no character or 'feel'. In contrast, place has a history. Place therefore, unlike space, is always unique. This place is not that place. The philosopher Edward Casey describes the difference like this: '"space" is the name for that most encompassing reality that allows things to be located within it ... "Place" on the other hand, is the immediate ambience of my lived body and its history, including the whole sedimented history of cultural and social influences and personal interests.'[26]

The observation made by many is that in our present age (modernity), space has overcome place. What does this mean? It really means that increasingly we have lost the uniqueness and specialness of places, in favour of the non-uniqueness of spaces. If this sounds abstract, we only need to think about the way that our high streets all look the same. You could be in Durham, Doncaster or Dartford and you will find the same shops, selling the same products. That's space overcoming place. Shopping centres embody this even more beautifully. The point is not to create difference and uniqueness; the point is to create familiarity and comfort. The human *need* for place is there – companies know that as humans we long for place – it's just that we can now be in control of creating this wherever we want. So we make this coffee shop, or computer store, exactly the same as the one closer to home. We gradually lose the distinctiveness of places in favour of manufactured spaces. Ex-mining communities struggling to find a sense of identity; generationally local communities priced out of housing stock in big cities; indigenous peoples losing their homes due to deforestation: each of these is a manifestation of the phenomenon that has been called 'the loss of place', which is seen to be true of modernity. Increasingly, we lose touch with the story that makes each place what it is.

Why or how this has happened is a different question. For

example, political theorists are interested in this phenomenon because of the ways it seems to be one aspect of our economic system.[27] A truly global economy thrives off the loss of place, essentially because space is easier to monetize. Place is invaluable, space is merely costly. What is interesting for our purposes, however, is to note how this loss of place is seen to be just one phenomenon of the wider reality that is modernity. For now, I want to focus on what are generally seen as two of modernity's core aspects: a sense of advancing away from tradition and a prioritizing of the individual and their choice. These are important because both have a huge impact on the way we think of place. First, as I said above, what makes a place a place is in large part its story and history, what has gone before. Thus, a move away from tradition – which I define as a set of stories or practices that are passed on – will inevitably mean a move away from place. Once we forget (or choose not to remember) a place's story, it stops being the place that it is and becomes just another space, open to whatever use we might imagine for it. But, second, we should also see the way in which stories are shared realities: they rely on others to be told and to be passed on. Thus, modernity's obsession with the individual and their choice makes it very difficult for the stories that make a place to have any real hold on us. What matters is not the story we grew up in, or consider ourselves to be part of, but the *story we choose to create for ourselves*. What we have then is modernity's two-pronged assault on the concept of place. Tradition is eroded, as are stories, leaving us devoid of the meanings that make places. If it is the individual who interprets and creates meaning, then the idea that places might 'just exist' – have value irrespective of our own use of them – is simply untenable. Once again, if this sounds like a purely theoretical claim, the reality is a very familiar one in our culture. Note, for example, the number of books, films or TV shows whose story is driven by a main character's desire to break free from what is presented as the overly traditional (and thus) restrictive confines of their context.[28] Such stories narrate the loss of place in modernity perfectly: the protagonist battles the givens of her place to create her own meaning, her own story and her own place. 'Let it go!' sings Elsa, in a true anthem of modernity.[29]

The theological pushback

The claim that is made in critiques of this phenomenon is that losing place leaves us deficient; that place is integral to what it is to be human. There has been a strong defence of place in much recent theology. Again, it is not my purpose to repeat these arguments in any depth. The claim that recurs is that there has been within the Christian tradition (scripture and Christian theology) a constant suspicion of what we might call universalizing, which does not first take into account particularity. In other words, Christianity has taken seriously real people in real places (particularity), rather than beginning with generalized truths. So the human story in Genesis begins not with 'humanity' – as either an amorphous whole or an ideal – but with Adam and with Eve. The story is set not 'on earth' but in Eden – a place – which is, in turn, described in some detail. This focus on place is a resounding theme throughout the scriptures: Eden itself is recapitulated in God's gift to Israel of the land, which in turn narrows in on Jerusalem and the temple, both of which become central to the New Creation in Revelation, where the whole show ends, not with 'the world', but in a definite place, a named city. All of it is particular: the story is for all, because it was for *them*; it is for the world, only in that it happened *here*. And standing at the very centre of it all is the incarnation. The saviour of all people is a Jew, born in Bethlehem and raised in Nazareth. God redeems his cosmos, not through universal ideals, but through flesh and blood, a human person in place. 'Can anything good come out of Nazareth?' asks Nathanael (John 1.46), and the answer to that question has shaped Christian thinking ever since.

This, I think, is the basis of what I suggest is a deep instinct about place within Christian theology, and indeed the instinct that I argue is most at play within the defenders of the parish considered here. Put simply, the instinct is to be *for* place; this sense that true to what it is to be human, not least a redeemed human, is to be in a place. Indeed, going further, I would argue that placelessness has come to be seen as the symptom par excellence of modernity's failings. It is the consequence of prioritizing individual choice above all other commitment; it marks the breakdown of community, a loss of memory, a loss of a sense of where one fits within the world. Ultimately, to lose place is to lose humility. Place humbles us because it situates us within a set of relationships and a story that is not of our own making ('This place existed long before I came to be, and will continue after I go').

For the theologian Willie James Jennings, place captures the sense of our being rooted and en-fleshed. It is, he writes, the mark of 'our creatureliness'.[30] In contrast, for Jennings our modern age is marked by a constant attempt at displacement: to pull human beings out of their connection with land and environment, and thus to turn place into space. We have witnessed, and witness, what Jennings calls 'the commodification of space' with a vision for 'a people freed to be anything they wish, enabled by marketability and consumer-identity building possibility'.[31] Such an understanding of place and modern space is integral to Jennings' claims about race identity. What the Christian tradition was able to do so devastatingly, he argues, was to remove the sense of a given connection to the land as the mark of our humanity, and instead replace it with the category of 'race'. What distinguishes people groups in this construct, therefore, is not local belonging, but these meta-categories of racial identity. And it is this ideology that in turn makes possible the imaginary space in which people can be uprooted and displaced (from their land, tradition, history). In other words, categorizing in this way – black, brown and so on – which is a feature of modernity, allows us to see people simply as 'types' of a universal humanity, rather than recognizing the fact that human persons are always woven inexorably to their places and are therefore fundamentally particular.

Jennings writes of how strange it now therefore seems to us that identity should be conceived of geographically. '[But] what if', he writes, 'it seemed strange, odd, and even impossible for you to conceive of your identity apart from a specific order of space – specific land, specific animals, trees, mountains, waters and arrangements of days and nights?'[32] It is this 'articulated connection to the earth ... a place-bound identity, a form of existence before or "below" race itself' that, therefore, 'comes under profound and devastating alteration with the age of discovery and colonialism'.[33] Jennings' call, therefore, is for a reconsideration of the doctrine of creation, from this basis of place identity. 'If Christianity is going to untangle itself from these mangled spaces it must first see them for what they are: a revolt against creation.'[34]

The assertion of modern space for Jennings, therefore, is essentially the assertion of the human will: we can make spaces whatever we want them to be. It is a manifestation of the arrogance of the human heart, living outside our creaturely confines, acting as God. This is what John Milbank means when he ends his defence of the parish by talking about the difference between 'endless possibility' and 'limited actuality'.[35] The former is the creed of modernity: we can make of our world whatever we wish, the only limit is our imagination! In contrast, it is the latter that is the more truthfully Christian instinct: we exist within the bounds of place and, far from being restrictive, these bounds are the very means by which we might find life.[36]

The fear of the critics of *Mission-shaped Church* and Fresh Expressions explored here is that the church might play into modern views of space, rather than working within this theological commitment to place. Here, therefore, is a church, and churches, that look and feel essentially 'modern'. If the parish is seen to establish churches (and a church) that have a field of responsibility, coverage, a connection to the past and a focus on the local and particular, then the loss of parish is seen to signify the move away from these. In view, then, are churches that are: Introspective – existing only to meet the needs (choices) of those who have chosen to belong, rather than those of the communities they sit within; Niche and homogenous – unable to say that they exist for all, existing only for targeted or selected networks and/or demographics; Thin – disconnected from Christian tradition and history, committed only to the now and an imagined future; Generic – shaped not by their locale, but by a standardized model of church (think Starbucks or McDonalds).

And so with these images of church on the horizon, it is deep into the parish church that these writers dig. The parish is 'a politically charged act of resistance to the forces of the age', assert Davison and Milbank, and my claim so far has been that for 'forces of the age' we could read 'placelessness'.[37] My task in the next chapter will be to explore this jump: the assumption that it is the parish that defends against this modern space. Before that, however, I do want to return to my initial claim about instincts, and make the observation that, irrespective of the way it is worked out, the instinct at least is a good one. There are good theological reasons why the church should be wary of the tendencies inherent in our cultural context to erode place. The argument I want to make is that this instinct for place is in fact an extremely deep one. What I suggest these defenders of the parish embody is a *love* of place.

For the love of place

The theologian Pete Ward has spoken about what he calls 'the affective gravitational pull of the church', and I think this is a helpful phrase for us here.[38] He writes: '"Affective" refers to the feelings and emotions the church imparts to us. These act as a force in our lives. The gravitational pull of the church is both doctrinal and experiential.' I want to take Ward's concept. However, rather than talking about church, I want to talk about the affective gravitational pull of *place*. Place behaves just like Ward thinks church can: it has a 'pull' on us. It is similar to what I have referred to throughout as an 'instinct', but Ward's use of 'affective' is important. 'Affective' captures the sense that this is about a feeling, or even mood, as much as it is about our thinking.

If there is one contemporary writer who highlights the way that place can act in this way, it is Wendell Berry, whose work is largely focused on the consequences of modernity's erosion of place for the sake of space. As John Inge picks up, Berry's work should thus be of keen interest to theologians grappling with place.[39] Within Berry's work we do find evidenced reasoning against placelessness – the consequences of loss of topsoil, urban poverty and systemic racism, for example[40] – however, Berry is really a poet before he is a scientist. His core argument is that our relationship with the world, with place, is dependent on an attitude rather than on doctrine or theory. He writes of the hope for humankind's relationship with creation:

> [It] requires that we make the effort to know the world and learn what is good for it. We must learn to cooperate in its processes, and to yield to its limits. But even more important, we must learn to acknowledge that the creation is full of mystery; we will never entirely understand it. We must abandon arrogance and stand in awe.[41]

Berry's work is pervaded by the sense of awe of which he writes here. Ultimately, according to him, there are two fundamentally opposed world views – 'two minds' – by which we can live in the world. And it is what he calls the 'sympathetic mind', in opposition to the 'rational mind', that best describes the instinct for place I see in the defenders of the parish. Thus, where the rational mind acts *upon* the world (it is the mind of modernity), the sympathetic mind responds to what is there. It is 'moved by' – and here is our word – '*affection* for its home place, the local topography, the local memories, and local creatures'.[42] The instinct about place is about an affection: a love of places in their uniqueness and particularity. We cannot in this sense rationalize our way towards place, we can only *know* it and choose to live within it. It is about home rather than house.

The writer Eugene Peterson – whose writing has in the past few decades become standard reading in pastoral care and spiritual formation across the spectrum of Christian expression – is undergirded by this dialectic between space and place to the extent that 'place' has been described as the central theme of his writing.[43] Peterson is in fact a stepping-stone from Wendell Berry, since Peterson himself notes his indebtedness to Berry. As he puts it, 'Whenever Berry writes the word *farm*, I substitute *parish*; the sentence works for me every time.'[44] For Peterson, what matters in the pastoral vocation is a certain rootedness, a willingness to stay put and be present here, in place. Such fixity is one of the core ways in which Christian vocation differs from the secular mindset or from contemporary American values which, for Peterson, can so easily become church values. 'Now is the time', he writes, 'to rediscover the meaning of the local, and in terms of church, the parish. All churches are local ... One of the pastor's continuous tasks is to make sure that these conditions are honored: *this* place as it is, *these* people in their everyday clothes.' And then, quoting Berry, the task as he sees it is to foster 'a particularizing love for local things, rising out of local knowledge and local allegiance'.[45] The affective pull of place runs throughout Peterson's work and in his writing there is a continued stress on particularity, locality and the need for a ministry defined by its permanence. His is not a romanticized version of place, however. Indeed, like many of the writers we have explored thus far, place is what it is precisely *because* of its complexity, even messiness. The opposite tendency, away from place, is therefore an escapism. Just as the prophet Jonah fled, so we too long to find a Tarshish; a ministry space of our own making.[46]

Four colours of the affective pull of place

Can we pin down what this affective pull of place consists of? As Berry's work suggests, this is a difficult task, since there is a certain abstractness to the pull of place. To state again, place is better expressed in poetry than logic. Among the theological writings around place, however, there are some common themes that occur, whether they directly address the parish or not. These themes, I suggest, offer a kind of palette, which gives some colour to the felt affective pull towards place. I want to highlight four of these themes. Affective pull towards place is about: particularity, complexity, connection to the past and permanence. What we should note is the way in which each of these themes depends upon a certain *feel* about place. Further, each is held through a contrast: it is only possible to explain what place feels like when we contrast it with its perceived absence.

Particularity

The first of the four is the richest since it is in many respects the basic shape of the affective pull of place that grounds the others. I have written above of the concern within Christian thought to avoid universalizing, without first going through particularity. This is what lies behind John Milbank, and Davison and Milbank, citing G. K. Chesterton's claim that we can only love, as it were, locally (rather than universally, or nationally).[47] That is to say, 'love of nation' is a vacuous concept unless what it really means is a love of one's garden or neighbourhood or indeed one's neighbour. Inge offers a lovely description of Berry's thinking when he says that 'devotion should thin as it widens'.[48] In Oliver O'Donovan's words: 'To love everyone in the world equally is in fact to love nobody very much'.[49]

The sense is that modern space does precisely the opposite. Rather than loving particularity, from within modernity we apply universal principles and forms from above. This is what George Ritzer in 1993 described as the process of 'McDonald-ization'.[50] It is the world of Starbucks, shopping malls and trading estates. In terms of geography, this valuing of particularity is often expressed in the term 'local'; there is a felt value to locality. The village, neighbourhood or housing estate matters in a way that the language of 'city' or 'region' simply cannot capture. However, this process of McDonaldization is deemed to happen at every level. Certainly at the level of cities, neighbourhoods and shops, but it is also felt as a more insidious tendency. Indeed, this overriding of particularity is held to affect the way in which we see one another. As we lose the distinctiveness of places, so too we begin to lose our sense of the distinctiveness of people. Place particularity is, therefore, about a deep sense that we need to protect a view of human *persons*. Thus, one of the features of the affective pull of place is a deep-felt aversion to treating people as objects or targets. It is little surprise then that it is often those who critique new forms of church who also have a wariness of language of numerical growth. So the argument goes: people are not an example of a type, nor are they to be *quantified* – as modernity sees space – but simply to be loved.

The theme of particularity is a central theme of Ben Quash's book *Found Theology*.[51] Quash's argument is that as Christians we live in the world through a constant to-ing and fro-ing between our *givens* (scripture, doctrines, church teachings and so on) and what is *found* (our experience of being human; what we discover as we go through life). It is these found aspects that Quash is especially interested in. His point is that God is continually opening us up to new findings, and thus the call is for us to receive these. Not imposing theories or principles in advance (that is, simply sticking with our givens, and trying to squeeze these new findings into preconceived categories) but receiving whatever and whoever we come across. The point is that these findings are *particular* and *unique*. In essence, it returns us to the sense of place as home; as something to be experienced from *within*, rather than explained from the outside. This is what lies behind Quash's own endorsement of the parish: if churches are to take seriously the uniqueness of people, then they must be open to receive place in its particularity. Place is always, as Andrew Rumsey argues, 'people-scaled'.[52] Quash makes explicit the link between our attitude to one another and place:

Every area of land is covered by a parish, and every resident of every parish – whether he or she is an Anglican or not – is someone to whom the Church has an obligation ... The parish and its priest enact a 'chaplaincy to place', not just a targeted ministry to those individuals who are signed up members of the institution. In these terms, no one ought to be regarded as just 'happening to be in the area'. Each person is to be treated as a significant 'finding'.[53]

Embracing the complexity of life

This second feature of the affective pull of place comes directly out of the first. Particularity entails messiness. That is, the process of imposing something from the outside has a sort of tidiness to it – a KFC drive-through can be built 100 miles away before being simply dropped into place – whereas dwelling in place is a complex business. To dwell in place is to put oneself at the mercy of the warp and weft of life. Behind much of the writing around place then is a certain felt sacramentality. Indeed, the connection of parish, place and sacrament is one feature of the Catholic instinct inherent within Anglicanism.[54] Sacrament captures the sense that God goes on meeting us through the particularities of human events, moments, objects and places: in the ordinariness of things. In Chapter 3, I shall qualify this idea somewhat, but for now it is worth saying that this felt sacramentality is the Christian expression of Berry's assertion that the physical creation is imbibed with mystery, and thus that our posture towards it must be one of awe. The affective pull of place is in large part an expression of this awe; a desire to situate oneself within the world rather than above it, to avoid the perceived controlling tendencies of modernity. There are two ways this is outworked. The first is that this affective pull of place is about valuing the 'civic' aspects of life alongside the 'religious'. Rumsey, for example, draws on Dietrich Bonhoeffer's idea of the church 'at the centre of the village' to make this point.[55] Taking place seriously seems to be about an aversion to 'sectarianism', avoiding the church becoming a 'holy-huddle' away from the aspects of everyday existence and all that is required for common life. It is the desire that the good news should reach into all spheres: politics, education, industry, housing, law and order, and everything else. Second, a longing for place has much to do with a desire to move into brokenness. There is a fear that what modern spatiality is essentially concerned with is *flight*: to find more and more effective ways to avoid the harshness of reality and live as unrestrictedly as possible. But the instinct for place is to move, not away from trouble, but more deeply into it. This plays out in the way in which we treat and value some of the places of our nation that can tend to be forgotten, something that Bishop Philip North, for example, has called our attention to in recent times, and which a number of significant reports have highlighted over the years.[56] The affective pull of place – expressed in the parish – is about a desire to be situated within the brokenness of the world when everything around us tries to pull us out of it.

Connection to the past

Place is, as I have said, largely constituted by history; a place is a site that has a particular story. One of the features of the affective pull of place is a longing to be connected with what has gone before. The critique of 'newness' comes through strongly in each of the three evaluations of Fresh Expressions explored in this chapter, and such newness is seen to be a strong feature of modernity. Modernity cannot value what has been, because it always has an eye on what can be; where there is room for more. Likewise, if place is space with story, then the valuing of space over place is really about the erosion of these stories. Once again, the narrative of escape plays out here. If the foundational unit of modernity is the individual and their choices, then the task is to become more free; that is, to move away from whatever has gone before. You are shaped not by the context – the place – you might have grown up in or now live in, instead you are to form your own identity. The pull of place, therefore, is a pull back into what has been, a sense that we are always conditioned by the past. It is a humility about one's situation in the world; that others have gone before me, and that I have far more to learn than to teach. In Christian terms, it is the sense that we encounter God in the long history of the church and God's activity in this place.

Permanence

The affective pull of place is about a longing for rootedness, to be located. This is a core part of the distinction I outlined earlier from David Goodhart, between 'Anywheres' and 'Somewheres'. For a Somewhere, Goodhart claims, place is a core feature of identity; one is who one is because one is *from* somewhere. In contrast, the Anywhere instinct is towards transience, and thus identity is constructed without recourse to place. The key distinction between these ways of being in the world is around fixity: whether or not one has been rooted somewhere and – importantly – imagines oneself to be rooted to this somewhere on into the future. The modern tendency can be marked by what I once heard a Methodist pastor describe as an 'addiction to destination': the best thing is always almost certainly happening somewhere else, and I therefore have an obligation to go and find it. The affective pull towards place then is about a longing to be committed to a place, to dwell here. Or, to use the scriptural language, to *abide*. As noted above, such abiding is a central theme of Eugene Peterson's writing, flowing out of his own experience of serving as a pastor to one church for almost three decades. Ben Quash also deals with this theme as it relates to place in his book, *Abiding*. Like Peterson, Quash draws on the *Rule of St Benedict* and its notion of stability, recognizing here a historical resonance with our contemporary tendency to flee.[57] We are too often, argues Quash, like modern-day 'gyrovagues' (monks who would wander from monastery to monastery), hoping that eventually someone or somewhere will meet our needs. In contrast to this, to dwell in place is to commit oneself to a boundary, to a limit, and thus give enough space to be changed. If rootlessness speaks of a dissatisfaction with self, then rootedness offers healing through self-giving. As Quash states, 'stability is intended to witness to our common humanity under God. It is about accepting rather than choosing one's neighbour ... it is, as one early Christian writer put it, a virtue we have "in common with God."'[58]

These are, I suggest, four features of the affective pull towards place that we see in much recent theology, and not least in the work of those who would seek to defend the parish. Place is held to offer particularity, complexity, connection to the past and permanence. I have used that language of affection since, to state again, there is a 'pull' towards place; we feel a longing for these things. In this sense, the defence of the parish is about something far deeper than expressible argument or quantifiable measure. Above all, I hope to have demonstrated that as well as being deep, this longing for a place is also *faithful*. There are good Christian reasons to feel like this about place, and the felt affective pull towards place might well, therefore, be one fruit of our discipleship; a result of our being formed by the Spirit of God. Christ at work within us pulls us towards place.

However – and it is the 'however' of this book – the pull to place remains just one instinct. And in that sense it is worthy of further reflection. First, it is just *one* instinct, and therefore it must be held alongside other, potentially as important and faithful, Christian instincts. Second, it is one *instinct*. Just as healthy instincts keep our body alive, so too we have words to describe someone who acts solely based on instinct. We might say that the process of growing in maturity is about becoming aware of our instincts and learning to manage them well. This is the task of this book. How might this instinct about place – this affective pull – be worked out in our current context? The assumption made by the defenders of the parish outlined in this chapter is that the instinct must necessarily result in the parish. I am sceptical of this claim, both because it tends to oversimplify the nature of place and the Christian story about place, but also because it makes too simple a leap from the instinct to the form of the parish. Out of this survey of the instinct for place, the questions I think we need to ask are: Might it not be at least possible that our longing for place will lead us to question as much as embrace the current system as we find it? Might there even be a drive for us to embrace other, non-parochial forms of church? In the next chapter I want to lay the groundwork for the type of conversation I think we should be having about the parish in our time; one in which we are able to hold apart the parish vocation from the parish structures.

Notes

1 John Day, 2019, *Homing*, London: John Murray.

2 Andrew Davison and Alison Milbank, 2010, *For the Parish: A Critique of Fresh Expressions*, London: SCM Press; Martyn Percy, 2008, 'Old Tricks for New Dogs: A Critique of Fresh Expressions', in *Evaluating Fresh Expressions: Explorations in Emerging Church*, Louise Nelstrop and Martyn Percy (eds), Norwich: Canterbury Press, pp. 27–39; John Milbank, 'Stale Expressions: The Management-Shaped Church', *Studies in Christian Ethics*, 21:1 (2008), pp. 117–28.

3 Davison and Milbank, *For the Parish*, p. viii.

4 Davison and Milbank, *For the Parish*, pp. 22, 27, 117.

5 Davison and Milbank, *For the Parish*, p. 7.

6 Davison and Milbank, *For the Parish*, pp. 93–116.

7 Davison and Milbank, *For the Parish*, p. 55.

8 Davison and Milbank, *For the Parish*, p. 49.

9 Davison and Milbank, *For the Parish*, p. 81.

10 Davison and Milbank, *For the Parish*, various places but especially, pp. 55, 64f., 68.

11 John Milbank, 'Stale Expressions'; emphasis original.

12 Percy, 'Old Tricks', p. 38. See Davison and Milbank, *For the Parish*, pp. 75–6.

13 See, for example, Donald McGavran, 1990, *Understanding Church Growth*, 3rd edn, Grand Rapids, MI: Wm B. Eerdmans.

14 Percy, 'Old Tricks', p. 34.

15 Percy, 'Old Tricks', p. 37.

16 Percy, 'Old Tricks', p. 37.

17 That the church is first and foremost to be different is highlighted by Davison and Milbank's definition of mission as: 'to unveil and reveal the Divine ordering of the world and the true humanity'. Davison and Milbank, *For the Parish*, p. 134.

18 Davison and Milbank, *For the Parish*, p. 80.

19 I use 'modernity' here to refer to the period in Western thought, culture, politics and economics since the Enlightenment of the seventeenth century and up to and including the present day.

20 Davison and Milbank, *For the Parish*, p. 86.

21 Davison and Milbank, *For the Parish*, p. 89.

22 Emma Thompson, 2021, 'Parish churches are a "spiritual NHS"', *The Telegraph*, 24 December.

23 As this argument relates specifically to the parish, see Andrew Rumsey, 2017, *Parish: An Anglican Theology of Place*, London: SCM Press, and Martin Robinson, 2020, *The Place of the Parish: Imagining Mission in our Neighbourhood*, London: SCM Press.

24 Thus, in the Greek, space as *spadion/stadion* (measurability and distance) and place as *topos* (bound and limit) or *chora* (ground of being or meaning). See Jeff Malpas, 'Thinking Topographically: Place, Space, and Geography', https://jeffmalpas.com/wp-content/uploads/Thinking-Topographically-Place-Space-and-Geogr.pdf, accessed 16.11.2022.

25 The language of space and place is controversial and there is little agreement within human geography as to the use of them. Complexity is added by the fact that writers frequently use the terms interchangeably, even to mean the opposite of how others have used them. If there is some agreement about the *nature* of place (if not the terminology), it is around the idea that place has something to do with lived and felt human experience, in contrast to space, which is neutral. As Philip Hubbard and Robert Kitchin claim, 'One thing that does seem to be widely agreed is that place is involved with embodiment' (Philip Hubbard and Robert Kitchin (eds), 2011, *Key Thinkers on Space and Place*, 2nd edn, London: SAGE, p. 6.) See on this point Tim Cresswell, 2004, *Place: A Short Introduction*, Oxford: Blackwell.

26 Edward Casey, 2001, 'Body, Self, and Landscape: A Geophilosophical Inquiry into the Place-World', in P. Adams, S. Hoelscher and K. Till (eds), *Textures of Place: Exploring Humanist Geographies*, Minneapolis, MI: University of Minnesota Press, p. 404.

27 See, for example, David Harvey, 1996, *Justice, Nature and the Geography of Difference*, Oxford: Blackwell.

28 This is not to reject the narrative per se. Not only is such an 'escape' from tradition liberating for many (and vital, in the case of, say, oppressive or abusive contexts), but is also often offered as an

appropriate critique of tradition; precisely the sort of critique I hope to offer in this book. The climax of many of these stories is the moment where those within the traditional context realize its restrictiveness and become less fearful. This is a very common theme in Disney films.

29 Disney's 2013 film, *Frozen*. The irony is that the film ultimately critiques the world view that the song expresses: Elsa learns what it means to live within the confines of her condition, and she chooses not escape, but taking hold of her vocation and the responsibility it entails.

30 Willie James Jennings, 2010, *The Christian Imagination: Theology and the Origins of Race*, New Haven, CT: Yale University Press, p. 293.

31 Jennings, *Christian Imagination*, p. 290.

32 Jennings, *Christian Imagination*, p. 40.

33 Jennings, *Christian Imagination*, p. 40.

34 Jennings, *Christian Imagination*, p. 248.

35 Milbank, 'Stale Expressions'.

36 Jacob's declaration at Bethel – 'Surely the LORD is in this place – and I did not know it!' (Genesis 28.16) – takes on a fresh meaning here. It is only by being in place that Jacob is able to know God. Rumsey uses this verse as the basis for his brilliant description of place. See Rumsey, *Parish*, chapter 1.

37 Davison and Milbank, *For the Parish*, p. 92.

38 Pete Ward, 'Blueprint Ecclesiology and the Lived: Normativity as Perilous Faithfulness', *Ecclesial Practices*, 2:1 (2015), pp. 74–90.

39 John Inge, 2003, *Christian Theology of Place*, Aldershot: Ashgate, pp. 127ff.

40 Each of these issues appears frequently in the smorgasbord that is Berry's writings. For a good introduction, see the essays collected in Wendell Berry, 2017, *The World-Ending Fire: The Essential Wendell Berry*, essays selected by Paul Kingsnorth, London: Penguin. Berry addresses the issue of racism specifically in 2010, *The Hidden Wound*, Berkeley, CA: Counterpoint.

41 Berry, 'A Native Hill', in *The World-Ending Fire*, pp. 1–36.

42 Berry, 'Two Minds', in *The World-Ending Fire*, pp. 178–201; emphasis added.

43 See Rodney Clapp's foreword in Eugene Peterson, 1993, *The Contemplative Pastor: Returning to the Art of Spiritual Direction*, Grand Rapids, MI: Wm. B. Eerdmans.

44 Eugene Peterson, 1994, *Under the Unpredictable Plant: An Exploration in Vocational Holiness*, Grand Rapids, MI: Wm. B. Eerdmans, pp. 131f.

45 Peterson, *Under the Unpredictable Plant*, pp. 129–30; emphasis original.

46 This is a central image in *Under the Unpredictable Plant*.

47 John Milbank, 'Stale Expressions'; Davison and Milbank, *For the Parish*, p. 158.

48 Inge, *Christian Theology of Place*, p. 131.

49 Oliver O'Donovan, 2004, 'The Loss of a Sense of Place', in Oliver O'Donovan and Joan Lockwood O'Donovan, *Bonds of Imperfection: Christian Politics, Past and Present*, Grand Rapids, MI: Wm. B. Eerdmans, pp. 296–320.

50 George Ritzer, 2015, *The McDonaldization of Society*, 8th edn, London: SAGE.

51 Ben Quash, 2013, *Found Theology: History, Imagination and the Holy Spirit*, London: Bloomsbury T&T Clark.

52 Rumsey, *Parish*, p. 67.

53 Quash, *Found Theology*, p. 13. The idea of 'chaplaincy to place' Quash gets from Timothy Jenkins. See Timothy Jenkins, 2006, *Experiment in Providence: How Faith Engages with the World*, London: SPCK.

54 The three critiques highlighted here each come from the 'Catholic' end of the CofE, as does Rumsey's book. Robinson, however, in *The Place of the Parish*, writes as an Evangelical, and for an Evangelical audience. His book thus marks the ways in which instincts transcend traditional lines, and often move between them. I see 'place', and the 'sacramental' theology that underpins it, as one of these and suggest that we are witnessing the ways this theology is becoming more prominent across the church, and churches.

55 Rumsey, *Parish*, pp. 53f.

56 See, for example, Archbishops' Council, *Presence and Engagement: The Churches' Task in a Multi-faith Society*, at https://www.churchofengland.org/sites/default/files/2018-10/gs1577-presence%20and%20engagement%3A%20the%20churches%27%20task%20in%20a%20multi-faith.pdf, accessed 16.11.2022; Church of England, 1985, *Faith in the City: A Call for Action by Church and Nation*, London: Church House Publishing.

57 See Ben Quash, 2012, *Abiding*, London: Bloomsbury, pp. 19–40, and Peterson, *Under the Unpredictable Plant*, pp. 18f.

58 Quash, *Abiding*, p. 35.

2

Disagreeing Well

In his book *Vexed*, James Mumford argues that in a polarized debate, what becomes all-important are one or two core issues that are fought over, and which become all determining of one's stance.[1] Mumford calls this 'package politics': take a stand on one issue and find another hundred thrown in for free. I have suggested that beneath the presenting response to the Church of England's affirming and establishing non-parochial churches is an instinct about place and modernity. Specifically, the claim is made that the church is called to embody the sympathetic mind; to value place over and against the overriding of place by space. Finally, I have suggested that deeper still is what I have called the affective pull of place: the emotional draw we feel towards what is local, tangible and bounded. The problem this chapter seeks to address is the way in which the depth of these responses – the gravitational pull – can tend towards a polarization in our thinking around the parish and new churches. It is clear from much that has been written about the parish in the past few years that it has come to serve as just such an artefact. It is a holder for the whole package deal.

Take as an example the 2021 incident that spawned its own hashtag. '#Limitingfactor' trended for a while in response to the comments of a senior church figure, Canon John McGinley who, when announcing the church's 'Myriad' programme to establish 10,000 new churches by 2030, appeared to describe church buildings, stipendiary ministry and college-based theological training as 'key limiting factors'.[2] His comments became a trigger event. It was clear from the reaction that his words tapped into something deeper, something that had clearly been felt by many for some time. 'Limiting factor' became synonymous for not only the Myriad project, but for a wider attitude or imaginary that was clearly perceived to be pervasive at the heart of the church. Take, for example, the words of the priest and cultural commentator Giles Fraser:

> The latest Great Leap Forward for the C of E looks like this. Get rid of all those crumbling churches. Get rid of the clergy. Do away with all that expensive theological education. These are all 'limiting factors'. Instead, focus relentlessly on young people. Growth, Young People, Forwards. Purge the church of all those clapped-out clergy pottering about in their parishes. Forget the Eucharist, or at least, put those who administer it on some sort of zero hours contract. Sell their vicarages. This is what our new shepherds want in their prize sheep: to be young, dumb, and full of evangelistic ... zeal.[3]

The phrase 'Great Leap Forward' – Chairman Mao's project of 'reform' – was borrowed from Martyn Percy, whose own two-part response is even starker than Fraser's. Not only Maoist China-like, but also an 'ecclesiastical Final Solution'.[4]

What are we to make of all this? Now, clearly not all of it is about the parish. From the examples cited thus far, there is a bigger story here. In particular, many of the responses homed in on the perceived gap between those 'on the ground' and those 'in head office'. That is to say, for many in the Church of England, there is a perception that the church has become unduly hierarchical, corporate and centralized: too many 'programmes' initiated from the top down and too much felt interference from those in a few key positions (so especially the archbishops and those at work in Church House). Like-wise, many of the responses expressed far deeper differences in theology and thus in missiology and ecclesiology. There is in many of them an overt suspicion of 'evangelicalism'; a feeling that the Church of England currently looks and feels too much like one flavour of the church.

So there is far more going on here than just the parish. But what I am interested in is the central role that the parish seems to play in it all; how it has become the artefact to which ecclesiological hopes are pinned. 'Save the Parish' in this sense became *the* response to the comments. And it is interesting then to read what exactly it is that these latest defenders of the parish believe it is that they are saving. The former Dean of Exeter Cathedral, Jonathan Draper, writes:

> [T]here will be no room in this brave new ecclesial world for those who see in the Christian faith a means of challenging the injustices, casualties, and myriad disasters of our world; no room for those who would like to see the church as more humane than the world – rather than the other way round … [This is] an abandonment of 2000 years of intellectual and spiritual development, of wrestling in public with the meaning and implications of the Christian faith, of trying to be the body of Christ in the world, the body of Christ for the world.[5]

There is a great deal to unpack here, but what in essence is assumed to be lost amid all of this is a Christianity that looks beyond itself; a church that focuses on the needs of the world, rather than its own agenda, and which, therefore, has to do the complex work of engaging faith in the public sphere. In Percy's words, 'The mission of the Church is a vocation to serve communities, not just convert individuals into members and grow that body exponentially.'[6] In view then is a church that has retreated, hiding behind its own walls and seeking only to enlarge. In other words, it is the church of modernity. This is ultimately what lies behind the terms that haunt the lines of these commentaries: 'managerialism'; 'corporate'; 'utilitarian'; 'mercenary'; 'statisticians at Church House'.[7] And here is the key point: in contrast to all this stands the parish; the holder for all that is not this. 'Limitingfactor-gate' is thus simply a contemporary example of the package politics Mumford names. To be 'for' the parish then – to wish to 'save' it – matters. Not simply because one cares about a certain historical institution or form, but more because one is rejecting a perceived 'other' form of Christianity.

But all of this is problematic. Of course, the fact that significant church and theological voices were willing to deploy language of genocide to describe an ecclesial strategy with which they disagree (or, at least, to lend tacit support to the claim) should immediately raise questions about the nature of the debate. Similarly, we should note the clumsiness of McGinley's comments, whatever it was he was intending to say. But the ferocity and/or laziness in the discussions around this issue are really symptoms of the deeper issue of polarized thinking that seems to pervade. The debate is problematic, not simply because it is damaging and hurtful – a poor witness to Jesus Christ and his body in the world – but because it suffers from the same issues as the packaged-deal reality that is polarized thinking. Just as happened with 'leave' and 'remain', so too through a classic turn and prestige, the parish has become more than merely an ecclesial system, even a historical fact, but is now a marker of one's convictions. A kind of ecclesiastical shibboleth. And, just as with the Brexit debate, the result is a loss of any nuance. Specifically, within the debate we witness a loss of the ability to separate out the object (in this case the parish) from the set of convictions or stance (the rejection of modernity and the longing for place) that become attached to it.

I suggest that this is precisely the danger of the debate as we find it today. To come back to where I ended the previous chapter, it seems to me that there are very good reasons why we should take seriously the pull towards place, and to see this pull as somehow central to the task of being the church. And it is this instinct I see as held deeply by those who are the most vociferous defenders of the parish. Indeed, the strength of that pull is largely what results in the depth of feeling expressed. However, the problem comes when that pull towards place is wedded indelibly to the particular form that is the parish structure. When this happens the choice is forced on us: are we for place and rootedness and therefore for the parish, or are we not? But this does not have to be the choice in front of us. As is often noted, there is a simplicity that sits on this side of complexity, and there is a simplicity that sits on the other side. The debate around the parish seems to fall into the mistake of assuming the former. Ironically, it might just be that one of the ways in which we *have* in fact allowed modernity to shape our ecclesiology is not so much in the content of the debate as in its nature, for this sort of polarized and reductionist thinking is one of the defining features of modernity.

What I want to do in the rest of this chapter is to show why and how I think this polarized thinking is a strange place to find ourselves as a Church of England. Of course, in one sense the Church of England is particularly susceptible to this way of thinking given that we are a collection of diverse ecclesiologies somehow held together in one church. We have always been Catholic *and* Reformed. However, diversity of approaches is qualitatively different from polarization. My claim here is that within the historical development of the Church of England, which led to the establishment of the Prayer Book (Thomas Cranmer) and the theology that emerged from the Elizabethan settlement (Richard Hooker), we find a particular theological method, which refused binary thinking and worked hard to ground church practices and structures in a certain theological pragmatism. I am of course aware that such a synthesis is a danger, and that any talk about a (singular) Church of England or even 'Anglican' approach is fraught with problems. I am therefore taking humble steps: what sort of thinking shapes those early conversations, which became imbibed in the Prayer Book?[8] My claim is that polarized thinking was never an option for a church that was seeking to offer 'common' prayer for the whole nation out of, and rooted in, the theological convictions of the Reformation. In what follows I first show why the parish is a far more complex reality than is often assumed within the debate, and that the thing itself – the parish – should be separated from the meaning attached to it. From here I want to explore Hooker and the Prayer Book to offer a more fruitful

way for us to proceed in our ecclesiological reflections as a
church.

The separation between the 'thing' and the 'meaning of the thing'

The cracks in the polarization of thinking around the parish
are evident in the earliest critiques made of the fresh expressions, which we explored in Chapter 1. What is noticeable here
is the divergence in the reasons given for the defence of the
parish. On the one hand, we have the position best represented
by Percy, who emphasizes the parish as establishing the church
in the world, for the common good. On the other hand, however, as in the case of John Milbank, are those who claim that
the parish is a defence of the church away from the world; that
is, that the parish enables the church to prophetically model an
alternative vision of what it is to be human. Thus, for Percy,
the parish system is the system that best sustains what he calls
'spiritual and social capital'.[9] Parish churches, he claims, are
'committed to deep local extensity', which promotes 'local commitment (that is, duty, obligation, etc.)'.[10] The parish church is
connected implicitly to its local community, and its very life
is defined by this connection. In contrast, however, Milbank's
support for the parish system has a distinctly less missiological
feel. For him, the parish is the system within which the church
is simply allowed to '*be* the body of Christ'.[11] To be human,
he claims, is to dwell specifically in one place and, thus, to
embrace our given particularity is more theologically true of us
than is the longing for endless universality. Further, the church
must necessarily be a body that embraces difference and, since
only a geographical space catches everyone equally, the church
must necessarily exist in a parochial form. One church in
one place is the best image we have of what Christian community should be: the 'assembly of humanity' can be most fully
realized in a system that puts particularity above universality,
and heterogeneity over homogeneity.[12] Thus, for Milbank, it is

the nature of the parish as a system rooted in geography that offers true unity in difference and refuses capitulation to the 'violence' of an attractional model which, in Milbank's view, only ever embraces, rather than works against, segregation. It is John Milbank's position that is the one more often encountered in *For the Parish*. As we saw, here the parish church is the church in resistance to the dehumanizing forces of our age, and it is 'the primary duty of the church *to be the church*'.[13] What we have then are two distinctive justifications for the parish. Where Percy posits the parish as the system that best connects the church *with* society, Milbank, and Davison and Milbank, see in the same system a church that is able to be *other* than society. Of course, both see the church as existing for the world; for John Milbank the church that is true to its calling, distinct from the world, is precisely the church that the surrounding society needs.[14] The fundamental contrast does remain, however. Where for John Milbank, and Davison and Milbank, the church's collusion with a culture of consumerism and choice is tragic because it will lead to the church being unable to offer any genuinely faithful alternative, for Percy the problem with consumerism is that it moves the church away from her sacrificial service on behalf of the world. Indeed, the distinction is perhaps best seen in the way in which they believe the geographical mapping itself to function. For Percy, the parish is most fundamentally a way of connecting the church to what is. It ties the church to the givens of people and place as it finds them. For Milbank, however, the parish is a Christian claim upon the land. 'In the European West', Milbank writes, 'terrain was first mapped out by the Church. And so we should never imagine that terrain is somehow more secular than it is sacred.'[15] Thus, the persistence of the parish model is, for Milbank, a commitment to this original claim; a way of the church refusing to jettison its vision of the life of the nation. We can put it, therefore, this way: where for Percy the parish is a work of responsiveness to existing reality, for Milbank it is a proactive action, which establishes a new reality.

What then can we say about this observation? In the first

instance, we must say that the parish is doing different things for each of these writers. Both are 'for the parish', but propose different justifications for being so. The parish thus acts as a sort of holder for the respective theological convictions and broader theological projects of each.[16] This is interesting because it suggests that there is at least the possibility that the link between the theological justification, and the parish structure itself, is not as obvious or given as the debate often assumes. The parochial system is concretized on a map but the theology that lies behind it is less so. We have then something of a 'gap' between, on the one hand, the 'thing' (parish) and, on the other, the 'meaning of the thing'. Clearly then, the claim that 'the parish' presents a uniform theological vision, which is in turn opposed to, say, 'networked' or 'attractional' church models, must be questioned. Might the logic work the other way round too? Could it be that the justification given for the parish *could* therefore lead to a different church form? This is surely the logical conclusion. Seen from John Milbank's perspective, for example, Martyn Percy's justification for the parish is misguided and thus, presumably, should in turn lead to a different ecclesial model. My point here is simply that we cannot assume that the parish 'means' something, which is then in contrast to other ecclesial structures that in turn mean something else. For the parish means different things for different people.

In contrast, one of the central claims of this book is that the parish system does not 'do' this or that, just as other ecclesial systems do not therefore do this or that. I should be clear: this is not the same thing as saying that ecclesial structure is irrelevant. The parish structure might well be the right form for the church to take; and we can certainly make an argument to that end. The problem comes, however, when we assume that a way of doing things (what we could call a church 'practice') necessarily holds within it a particular theological commitment, in such a way that any move away from that practice is therefore held to be a rejection of that theological commitment. Instead of this we must honestly ask the question that has been lying in the background to this book, and which the distinction between Milbank and Percy's respective defences of the parish necessitate: What if the practice (the parish structure) is not in fact doing what the theological commitment is wanting it to do? In other words, once the meaning of the thing is loosed from the thing itself, the conversation suddenly becomes richer. Instead of asking, Parish system, yes or no? we are able to ask, What must the church look like if it took the commitment to place seriously?

Much recent theology has sought to make sense of this apparent gap between what I have called the thing and the meaning of the thing; that is, between our practices and the theological meanings we assume for them. Take, for example, the work of the Roman Catholic theologian Nicholas Healy.[17] Healy is a helpful conversation partner here, because his starting point is so emphatic: practices are vital. His is thus a helpful corrective to one possible reading of what I have been saying up to this point, namely that practices are secondary to, and divorced from, ideas; that we could start with a theological idea (in this case, say, the principle that place matters), and then sort of find practices that serve this end. But Healy, as a wise theologian, knows that this is a weak view of practices. He is clear that our practices – indeed the very churches that we establish – speak volumes, telling of Christ, and of his gospel, and not only to the world, but perhaps more importantly, to us Christians. In this way, and following the likes of Stanley Hauerwas and others, Healy is clear that practices should be registered as *formative* actions. For these thinkers, practices are not so much the *result* of our thinking, as the very tools that shape that thinking. In terms of the parish then, we could say that the parish as a practice is significant because it shapes us in a certain way of seeing the world which, if we lost it, would thus be a detriment to our Christian imagination. The danger perceived by these defenders of the parish is therefore that if we lose the parish we will simply be shaped by other practices; that attractional church, for example, will turn us away from place to our choices and consumer freedom. So

Healy is not downplaying the importance of practices, whether that is our liturgies, our gatherings or our church forms. Healy recognizes this and affirms it. Structure matters. But – and it is this 'but' that Healy is so keen to explore – what we know from our own experience is that our practices do not always do the things we assumed they would do. And this is the 'gap' that I think we must take seriously in our discussions around church structures.

Healy's criticism then is of theological accounts of church practices that fail to offer an adequate account of human agency. As he puts it, 'practices are not mere behaviour patterns; they are actions performed by human agents'; and as such, in considering the value of any practice, we must reflect upon the intentionality of the actor performing it or, in church practices, of the 'recipient'.[18] His point is that in our understanding of church practices we must recognize that these practices are complex. That there is not a smooth line between practice and conviction and back again. As an example, Healy draws upon the practice of signing oneself with holy water as one walks into a church. In each instance and for each actor the practice is the same, however the intentionality or understandings of such an action may vary wildly between them. What if, Healy asks, the intentions behind the act are misguided (based on superstition, maintaining sectarian boundaries, or on guilt)?

> In such a case, performing the practice would not contribute to the formation of my Christian character, but would instead strengthen my *non*-Christian identity. Thus what, abstractly described, is a perfectly good practice from within a Roman Catholic construal, may concretely be a substantially different practice, even a 'socially established' and 'internally consistent' counter-Christian one.[19]

This is the sort of question I want to ask of the practice that is the parish (or indeed non-parish, such as church planting or pioneering a fresh expression). Is this practice serving to form us more in the likeness of Christ – as individuals and as a church

– or is it not doing that and, possibly, doing the opposite? The point Healy is making is that the practice alone cannot bear the weight of that answer. That is, it is not enough to say, 'Such and such a practice does x, and therefore so long as we are doing that practice we will be doing x and thus all will be well' (in our case: 'The parish does x, therefore so long as we do the parish we are doing x'). This doesn't work because – as Healy's illustration exemplifies – the practice might be enacted in such a way that it ceases to do what it was originally intended to do. There is then an underlying polemic in Healy's work: we must make sense of our practices within the real 'concrete' world, where human beings make actual decisions and think and behave in all sorts of complex ways.

To state again, Healy's claim is not that practices must serve our ideas; that we can dismiss practices easily once they have stopped 'functioning' as we want them to. To return to the example of holy water, Healy's point is not that we should therefore reject this practice. As he states, there are very good theological reasons in Roman Catholic theology for why this is a vital activity. Rather, it is that we must at the very least wrestle with how this activity is being performed and received; that the 'appropriate intentions and construals'[20] really do matter. This then is the balance: given practices (in this case, the parish) are indeed formative. It does matter what form our churches take, because all of this forms us as Christians. We do not merely learn how to be Christians in a discipleship class; we are 'taught' by the church itself. And yet we must recognize that all of these practices are continually in danger of being either practised, or appropriated, wrongly. Perhaps the biggest danger here, of course, is that the original intention of the practice has become lost, or is so 'implicit' that the meaning has become forgotten. This is what happens when, for example, a parish church loses explicit connection with its locale or when its congregation ceases to be in any sense representative of the surrounding community. Here, the fact that this is a parish church, and the parish was always about locality, is to all intents and purposes an irrelevance. The parish structure is no protector against the reality that this church has ceased to be in any real sense rooted in its place; is now just as detached as the imagined displaced fresh expression. But so too new churches. It is totally conceivable that a new church is started whose founding vision is to 'reach the last, the lost and the least' and yet which in its activity ceases to model this in any real sense. In both cases the church form cannot disguise the fact of a lack of local engagement; both have appropriated and construed their form wrongly. There is a phrase that has become common in leadership training that 'culture eats vision for breakfast', and I think in essence Healy would agree.

And so the balance must be held. Between a valuing of practices and church forms as formative, and the obvious fact that we must continually evaluate these practices and forms to ensure they are doing what we hoped they should. To come back to the language with which I began, it is a diligence in theology to hold apart the thing (practice) and the meaning of the thing; at least just long enough to allow us to assess the thing properly. To do so is not to reject the practice, but is instead to take it seriously.

A Church of England way of thinking

Healy's claims should not come as any surprise to those of us in the Church of England. Arguably it is a wrestling with this particular expression of the relationship between practice and theological instinct that has shaped much of our ecclesiology. The legacy of being a Reformed Catholic church is that often the theological questions that arise for Anglicans will concern the nature of our practices and, furthermore, such questions will need to be answered in a way that refuses to collapse the practice and theological conviction into one another. In the theological story of the Church of England's emergence, therefore, we witness a continual wrestle to hold God's freedom as central (the Reformation instinct) while making sense of the inherited catholic practices that were held to be so valuable to a majority of English people. In this way, the Church of England in its settled form can be seen as a mature theology of practice. As Rowan Williams puts it, this church, '[refuses] to bind God too closely to material transactions', but rather highlights 'the free activity of God sustaining and transforming certain human actions done in Christ's name'.[21] His point is that the Church of England has sought to value church practices and forms by recognizing their formative power and yet has wanted to avoid tying God, and God's activity, too tightly to them. God is free to form and shape his church as he wills, and our practices cannot and should not be definitive of this. Practices are therefore relativized, only not on the basis of functionality (that is, 'do they work?') but theologically. So the critical question to ask of every practice is this: How is God working through this practice so as to bring his church to fullness?

For Williams, Richard Hooker's critique of the Roman doctrine of transubstantiation can be understood precisely in these terms. According to Williams, what Hooker does so brilliantly here is to stress the 'effects' of the sacraments, as opposed to the precise manner of their working. For Hooker, it is God who gives himself to us in the Eucharist; this *is* the sacrament and where its power lies. Accordingly, any attempt to systematize, or overly explain, the *manner* of this – say by claiming that the sacrament's power is dependent upon the bread and wine *being* Christ – will necessarily detract from the freedom of God in the act. According to Hooker, it binds God within a particular logic and reasoning; transubstantiation is more 'plain than true' as Hooker puts it.[22] Williams describes Hooker's position:

It is not ... that Christ's presence needs somehow to be 'in' the bread and the wine before we receive them; the bread and the wine are vehicles of Christ's action to make us partakers of his life, and any further analysis of how this might happen is at best irrelevant and at worse impious.[23]

For Williams then, there is something foundational here for the Church of England in the way it makes sense of its given practices. In Hooker's understanding the sacraments are God given – 'a secret and sacred gift' – performed by (finite) human beings.[24] This is not, again, to make practices secondary. Hooker is not saying that we could do communion through any substance (packet of crisps and a Coke anyone?) simply because we believe God can choose to work however he wishes to. The point isn't that God's freedom devalues our performance of practices, and at no point does Hooker allow practices to become dispensable (that is, because God is free to move however he wants to, we shouldn't therefore worry too much about what forms our worship, or our churches should take). Indeed, such a move he sees as the particular failure of his Puritan interlocutors, who were all too ready to assume that sticking tightly to repeated practices was a form of works righteousness. Rather, for Hooker, God gives himself to work in this practice and so the particular act is itself vital. Yet if it is to remain a gift of grace, then it must remain fully God's act.[25] The delicate balance Hooker is trying to strike here is made explicit in his claim that a sacrament must consist of three parts. First, there is the gift of grace (that is, what God is doing in the sacrament); second, the physical element that signifies the grace (bread and wine); and third, the word that expresses and explains what has been done. It is then the relationship of the three things – distinct but held always together – that is crucial: God's activity, the thing itself (act of Eucharist) and the explanation of the thing.[26] For Hooker, it is the fact of the relationship between God's action and our action (or better, our participation in the acts he has given us) that allows for these to be held alongside one another. Sacraments are those acts, 'the use whereof is in our hands, the effect in His'.[27]

Two interrelated points can be drawn from this reading of Hooker's sacramental theology, both of which share something of Healy's concern about our practices. First, it should be clear that Hooker and Healy share common ground in their concern about tying together meaning and practice. What we find in Hooker is a rejection of two extremes: he is wary of overbearing the sacrament with interpretation, and yet he wants to avoid seeing the sacrament as *itself* the meaning. If we are to receive Christ in the Eucharist, then how the Eucharist is explained to us, and how we receive it, really does matter.[28] What is important then is the way in which Hooker carefully navigates this relationship, which avoids a collapse of the signified (the thing) into signified (the theological meaning).

Second, an important outworking of this relationship for Hooker is the need for words of explanation. For Hooker, no matter how tightly we hold the relationship between physical element or performance, and the grace that is bestowed, there is within their performance a need for more: a need for it all to be explained and made clear. Once again, the relationship between the two is always of a particular arrangement. Hooker was not a 'memorialist'; the sacrament is more than merely a sign or a teaching aid. However, he thinks that the real presence of Christ needs expounding if we are to receive the grace that God promises to give us through it. This is the purpose of the liturgy and the spoken word. As Hooker puts it, 'the one [the words of explanation], might infallibly teach what the other [the thing or performance] do most assuredly bring to pass.'[29]

Sacraments and church structure are clearly very different things, and it would be incorrect to assume that what Hooker says about the sacraments he would also say about the form of church structure. Rather I am here following Williams in identifying within Hooker's arguments around sacraments something of a type of 'Anglican' reasoning. Within Book Five of Hooker's *Laws*, there is something of a more general 'Church of England' approach, which above all sees practices as gifts, the effects of which are God's grace. We must take practices seriously, recognizing that as good gifts to us, we receive God's blessing to us when we perform them. However, we must also note that practices do not work like magic: that humanness must be taken into account. Thus, the way in which we perform these practices, the way we understand them, the way they are explained to us, the way we integrate them into the rest of our following after Christ, all of this matters. Indeed, it is precisely this conviction that lies at the heart of Cranmer's formation, and subsequent re-formations of the Book of Common Prayer. In in its opening section, 'On Ceremonies', for example, we see the claim made that practices are not faultless; they might in fact – either by intention or ignorance – lead away from grace rather than towards it. The gift is not a given. Thus, the BCP holds Hooker's line between a rejection of practices on the basis of theological liberty, and an adoration of the practice itself. The contrast is not between practices or no practices, but rather ceremonies that are 'dark [or] dumb' and those that are 'so set forth that every man may understand what they might mean, and to what use they do serve'.[30]

Back to the parish

It is here that we find, therefore, a good theological basis from which we might assess the debate around the parish system. As a repeated practice through which we have seen God work, the parish system must be a necessary starting point in the Church of England's ecclesiological thinking. In other words, we cannot assume that because God is free to work however he wishes to, this received practice can therefore be dismissed. To do so would be to assume the position of God; a form of ecclesiological arrogance. This is indeed a temptation for us as people shaped by modernity: to assume that we now have the answers, answers that, necessarily, our ancestors could not possibly have seen. However, at the same time, we must reject the possibility that the parish structure as a form through which God has worked and does work is therefore beyond assessment. Here we tie God not to our own new ideas, but to the form itself. Instead, the Prayer Book and Hooker's arguments – picked up by Healy – should lead us to wise and realistic assessment of the practice. I think Hooker in particular would question the way in which the parish has become idolized in certain quarters, not because he is a 'pragmatist' – as some have tried to paint him – but because he would be suspicious of this overly simplistic account of human activity and church form. He would not be surprised by the possibility that the structure might not live up to the high ideals bestowed on it by its defenders. What is necessary, therefore, is a proper accounting of the relationship between the practice itself (the parish system) and the meaning of that practice. My claim is that the critics of fresh expressions highlighted in the previous chapter do not do this, but rather too readily conflate the two things.

Might the moves within the Church of England to support and encourage non-parochial forms of church be understood, following the pattern of the BCP, to be part of the assessment, re-evaluation and clarifying of the parish system? I suggest that they might be, or at least that there is no reason why they could not. Once we acknowledge the separation of signifier and signified, a debate opens up about the potential for other non-parochial forms to embody the principle; that is, the vocation to presence. My critique of the approaches of Davison and Milbank, Percy and John Milbank at this juncture is not that they are blind to reality (though certainly the lack of empirical observation in their accounts does leave them somewhat deficient), but that they attribute too much value to the system itself. Again, what I want to challenge is the formula, used in varying forms throughout many of the defences of the parish that critique new forms of church, that 'Fresh expressions or church planting results in x, where the parish leads to y.' Such a formula implies that the system itself *does* something. I hope to have shown that, at least in Anglican reflections on praxis, there is an unease about this sort of language because of the awareness that practices or systems are not in themselves sufficient. The choice is not between different systems, but rather between the desire to be faithful in our practices or not. This is the challenge of receiving traditions, as Alasdair MacIntyre argues. In the case of the Church of England's ecclesiology, the task is to seek to find systems and patterns of ministry that best allow the church to be what it is called to be. Put differently, it is to continually push our church forms that they might better signify the principle for which they exist.

Starting in the middle

In saying that we hold apart the vocation and the structures, I am aware of the danger of imagining that we can start with a blank canvas, stating the vision, and painting from there. As though we could carve through the complexity of the parish structure as we have it and find some way of doing things that will solve all. However, and to paraphrase Rowan Williams' now frequently cited claim, we are always beginning in the middle of things.[31] We do not start from scratch in our think- ing about ecclesiology, strategy or anything else: the parish structure is what we have received; it is where we start from. I think the problem with *Mission-shaped Church* and some of the earliest fresh expressions theology that surrounded it, was that it seemed to want to establish an ecclesiology *ex nihilo*, bypassing what was received in the structure and the tradition. I understand this instinct, and there is a case to be made that every healthy system or institution needs this kind of thinking to propel the conversation forward. In that sense, *Mission-shaped Church* and Fresh Expressions was a success. The challenge for those of us who are in the 'second wave' of this reimagining since then (third wave, fourth wave, maybe?) is to make sense of it all from where we are.

As Andrew Rumsey argues, the parish (as a structure) has been a formative practice; the vocation to presence has, as it were, been carried within the system. We should therefore be wary of imagining that we might somehow jump outside it, simply clinging to an ideal of presence. The structure that sets each church within an area of responsibility matters because it has gifted us a way of imagining our relationship to the life of the nation. Thus, the structure may not be perfect – it may not even be 'working' – but the answer is not to reject structure altogether. Instead, *we need structures that will allow presence in place to happen in our context.* This is the challenge we face. Before moving on to addressing this task explicitly, however, we must reckon with the nature of place itself. If place is simple, then the task is simple. If place is complex, however – and I think it is – then the vocation to presence will demand fresh thinking. It is to the nature of place as a complex reality that I turn next.

Notes

1 James Mumford, 2020, *Vexed: Ethics Beyond Political Tribes*, London: Bloomsbury Continuum.

2 See 'Leader Comment: "Key Limiting Factors"', *Church Times*, 9 July 2021.

3 Giles Fraser, 2021, 'The Church is Abandoning its Flock', *Unherd*, 08 July, at https://unherd.com/2021/07/the-church-is-abandoning-its-flock/, accessed 03.09.2021.

4 Martyn Percy, 2021, 'The Great Leap Forward: The New Politics of Ecclesionomics for the Church of England', *Modern Church*, at https://modernchurch.org.uk/martyn-percy-the-great-leap-forward-part-one-the-new-politics-of-ecclesionomics-for-the-church-of-england, accessed 01.03.2022.

5 Jonathan Draper, 2021, 'Limiting Factors: the "Myriad" Initiative and the Future of the Church', *Modern Church*, at https://modernchurch.org.uk/limiting-factors-the-myriad-initiative-and-the-future-of-the-church, accessed 03.09.2021.

6 Percy, 'The Great Leap Forward'.

7 See 'Save the Parish' conference video at St Bartholomew the Great, 2021, 'Save the Parish', *YouTube*, 3 August, https://www.youtube.com/watch?v=_ZSmNuVKRXY, accessed 03.09.2021.

8 It is important to be aware of the dangers of talking about an 'Anglican' mode of reasoning or approach to theology as if it were (and ever was) a monolithic entity. There is an important revisionist account of Anglican history that needs to be heard, one that shows, for example, how the historical reality of the English Reformation is more complicated than the descriptor 'Anglican' can suggest. See, for example, the essays in Mark Chapman, Sathianathan Clarke and Martyn Percy (eds), 2016, *The Oxford Handbook of Anglican Studies*, Oxford: Oxford University Press. I use 'Anglican' here, therefore, not

to imply a historical fact, but rather according to Rowan Williams' 'reasonably generous definition': that type of theological approach best demonstrated in Hooker and in the Prayer Book. See Rowan Williams, 2004, *Anglican Identities*, London: Darton, Longman & Todd, p. 3.

9 Martyn Percy, 2008, 'Old Tricks for New Dogs: A Critique of Fresh Expressions', in *Evaluating Fresh Expressions: Explorations in Emerging Church*, Louise Nelstrop and Martyn Percy (eds), Norwich: Canterbury Press, p. 132.

10 Percy, 'Old Tricks', p. 126.

11 John Milbank, 'Stale Expressions: The Management-Shaped Church', *Studies in Christian Ethics*, 21:1 (2008), pp. 117–28; emphasis original.

12 John Milbank, 2009, *The Future of Love*, London: SCM Press, p. 273.

13 Andrew Davison and Alison Milbank, 2010, *For the Parish: A Critique of Fresh Expressions*, London: SCM Press, p. 82; emphasis original.

14 It is this formulation – that it is only out of her difference that the church offers anything to the world – that is more fully fleshed out by Davison and Milbank. They unpack, in a way John Milbank does not, for example, how the parish church might offer value to local common life. See *For the Parish*, pp. 170–208.

15 Milbank, 'Stale Expressions'.

16 The differences between these two perspectives, which lead to the differing conceptions of the parish, are made explicit by Martyn Percy in his book, *Engaging with Contemporary Culture*, in which he outlines his own cultural theology as a contrast to the movement of Radical Orthodoxy, of which John Milbank is a central part. In simple terms, for those within Radical Orthodoxy, the core Christian claim is that God is 'all in all', which results in a complete denial of any divide between 'sacred and secular'. There is thus no 'bit' of the world that is called 'Christian', that sits alongside another bit called 'secularism'. Rather the Christian claim about the world is a claim about the whole reality – all reality exists in God, under Christ – and thus Christian claims about the world must take logical precedence. Percy is critical of this, since he feels it refuses to hear or respond to what is given in the world, outside what is explicitly 'Christian'. Their respective views of the parish are thus an expression of this: is the parish simply a Christian naming of place (Radical Orthodoxy) or is there an existing 'secular place', which the church responds to (Percy)? See Percy, 2005, *Engaging with Contemporary Culture: Christianity, Theology and the Concrete Church*, Aldershot: Ashgate, especially pp. 66–70.

17 See, for example, Nicholas Healy, 2000, *Church, World and the*

Christian Life: Practical-Prophetic Ecclesiology, Cambridge: Cambridge University Press; Nicholas Healy, 'Practices and the New Ecclesiology: Misplaced Concreteness', *IJST*, 5:3 (2003), pp. 287–308.

18 Healy, 'Practices and the New Ecclesiology'.

19 Healy, 'Practices and the New Ecclesiology'.

20 Healy, 'Practices and the New Ecclesiology'.

21 Williams, *Anglican Identities*, pp. 2–3.

22 Richard Hooker, 1888, *Laws of Ecclesiastical Polity*, Book V, lii, in *The Works of that Learned and Judicious Divine Mr. Richard Hooker*, John Keble (arr. and ed.), 3 vols; 7th edn, rev. by R. W. Church and F. Paget, Oxford: Clarendon Press, at http://oll.libertyfund.org/titles/hooker-the-works-of-that-learned-and-judicious-divine-mr-richard-hooker, accessed 23.01.2016.

23 Williams, *Anglican Identities*, p. 28.

24 Hooker, *Laws*, Book V, l.

25 'For of the sacraments, the very same is true which Solomon's wisdom observeth in the brazen serpent, "He that turned towards it was not healed by the thing he saw, but by Thee, O Saviour of all."' Hooker, *Laws*, Book V, lvii.

26 Indeed, by emphasizing the relationship, Hooker can sound contradictory at points: 'they [the sacraments] really give what they promise and are what they signify' sits with, '[the sacraments] contain in themselves no vital force or efficacy' (*Laws*, Book V, lvii).

27 Hooker, *Laws*, Book V, lvii.

28 We might think, for example, of Paul's admonishment to the Corinthians (1 Corinthians 11) about receiving communion properly; clearly for Paul, simply receiving is not the only thing to be done, and it may in fact lead to curse rather than blessing.

29 Hooker, *Laws*, Book V, lvii.

30 The Church of England, 2004, The Book of Common Prayer, Cambridge, Cambridge University Press, p. xii.

31 Rowan Williams, 2000, *On Christian Theology*, London: Blackwell, pp. xii–xiii.

3

Place Isn't What it Used To Be

Human beings are ... restless creatures; they cannot remain
stationary in one room for more than twenty-four hours
without going stir-crazy. The problem is our stationariness,
not the singleness of the room.[1]

There is a saying, attributed to Martin Luther, that the world
is like a drunk person on a horse: just as he swings himself
back from falling off one side, so then he falls off the other. I
think this is a helpful way of imagining how we tend to think.
In our correcting, we are prone to overcorrection. My sense
is that theological thinking about place has been a bit like
this. I have argued that there has been a necessary and vital
reassertion of the importance of place in theological thinking
in recent times. As I have claimed above, much of this has been
a reaction against modernity; a call for the church to embrace
the scriptural witness of place, and the beauty of our tradition,
against the dehumanizing erosion of place that marks our time.
And to do this, the theological writing has thus pressed hard
in the direction of place as fixed and bounded. We saw this in
Chapter 1. Here the defence of place was about rootedness in
contrast to flux and flow; it was about locality and particularity. But my claim is that the theological pushback – and
especially as this has pulled in the issue of the parish – has
tended to overcorrect in the opposite direction. Specifically,
such a theology (and resulting ecclesiology) has overempha-
sized the sense of place as static and fixed, over and above the
view of place as changing and complex. This in turn has left
us with a somewhat deficient ecclesiology in the church, one

that is able to affirm the importance of place but struggles to find ways of engaging with place as it changes. This matters, because this sense of flux is not only the way in which many in our world experience place (think Anywheres), but it is also, at a conceptual level at least, full of truth. What lies behind the sense of disconnect with place that is experienced in many of our parishes is a symptom of this fact. We must be able to make sense of the way place changes as much as its fixity.

In this chapter, I want to engage with the language of space and place as it is understood within fields outside theology, and especially within human geography. My purpose here is not to try and fill in a perceived gap in the theology with material from elsewhere. Rather it is to use another discipline to help shed light on what I think has always been implicit within scripture and the Christian tradition but which in our defences of place we have been prone to miss. In the second half of the chapter I shall therefore turn explicitly to consider what we might say theologically about place as unsettled as much as settled.

Space and place and holding the tension

I showed in Chapter 1 that the theological reassertion of place tends to rely on the distinction between space and place. This is a helpful contrast, and it makes the point well. But what is interesting to note is the way in which within fields outside theology, and especially within human geography, the goal has been not so much to hold apart space and place, but to explore the ways they interact.[2] What do I mean by this? Essentially, geographers have been wary that in reasserting place in contrast to space we assume that because space is about choice and endless possibility, place therefore tends to be static and unchanging. In this way, human geographers have argued that modernity's view of space does have some basis in truth: that place can and does change, and that we are a part of effecting that change. This is the aspect, which in their overcorrection,

I think theological defenders of place have often missed, not least those who seek to defend the parish and the importance of 'locality'.

Take, for example, one recent book by Martin Robinson, *The Place of the Parish*.[3] In his book, Robinson draws on the work of Doreen Massey, a feminist geographer, to demonstrate the ways we as humans are formed and shaped by the places in which we dwell. And he is right in so much of this. Massey, following on from the likes of Henri Lefebvre, does want to show that humans don't simply create places, but that places create us; that there really are places, and these places exist whether we are there or not, and they existed before we came to be there. Robinson thus uses human geography to show that it is impossible to be a human without being in place; that all our thinking and acting is shaped by the places where we were born, grew up and now dwell (I am who I am because of where I am and have been). And he goes on from here to argue that, therefore, churches must take place seriously, becoming rooted in their local places. And yet what Robinson seems to miss is where Massey then takes her argument. Massey in her work is always wary of the lazy conclusion drawn from the fact that places shape us, namely that therefore places must be unchangeable things into which we humans must simply fit. Instead, she challenges what she calls the 'search after the "real" meanings of places', or a place's 'authentic character'. Such a longing, she argues, is 'a response to desire for fixity and for security of identity in the middle of all the movement and change'. No matter how bounded, how seemingly rooted in history, no place ever has an 'unproblematic identity'.[4] In other words, it is a mistake to think that a place is as it is for all time, as though there was some basic essence of this place that we could hold on to amid the flux and change of the world. As if this place *is*, for all time, 'ex-mining community', 'commuter town' or 'deprived estate'.

Massey's concerns arise from her commitments as a feminist thinker. For Massey, there is something about women's experience (and others' whom she would recognize to be marginalized) that should lead us to question the claims people make about the nature of place as settled and unchanging. Place conceived of as given and static is, she fears, necessarily non-progressive; a tool for maintaining a status quo. Massey's work is an attempt to work out how place really does function for us and our communities. How places change over time, how places connect to other places, how we give as well as receive meaning from places, how being 'in place' can mean oppression as well as liberation.

Place as bounded openness

One geographer who offers a helpful language for our discussion is the Australian writer Jeff Malpas. Malpas is stern in his rejection of modern conceptions of space, which see place as neutral terrain into which we bring meaning by our actions and choices. For Malpas, modernity 'can be understood as characterised by the attempt to abolish the limits on the human, to transcend the bounds imposed by place, to open up a realm of unrestricted spatiality'.[5] And to all this, Malpas offers a firm 'no'. We humans are bound to place; it is not simply the neutral ground upon which we can construct our identity, like the hardware on which we run our personalized operating system. There really is such a thing as place, and each place exists prior to my being there and long after I am gone. A place has a unique character and, as such, it shapes us. A key word for Malpas is 'boundary'. Every place is 'bounded' in this way; it is distinct and separate from other places. One place affects me in a unique way, and it is not the same in another place: the street, neighbourhood or city that we love really is distinctive, and is not the same as another.

And yet Malpas is alive to the overcorrection. For he is no less critical than Massey of any attempt to find the 'fixed' character of a place, or of arguments that rely on treating a place as having an obvious identity that transcends time. He writes:

[Such] arguments typically rely on treating place in a way that actually goes against the character of place itself: they tend to disregard the way place is itself bound up with both identity and difference as well as with plurality and indeterminacy.[6]

Identity *and* difference. This is the point. Place is settled, *and* it changes. For Malpas, the point is not to reassert place in a way that leaves place as fixed and static, but rather to show how place is always at once both bounded *and* what he calls 'open' ('bounded openness').[7] And it is this definition of place – as bounded openness – that I wish to carry forward in what follows. Places are 'bounded' – constant, definable, objective and real – but also 'open' – ever in flux, and formed in their relationship with other places. Both extremes of the spectrum must therefore be rejected, and there is always the tendency for us to lean too hard one way or the other and fall off the horse the other side.

The characteristic of place as bounded openness

One experience explains what I think Malpas means by describing place as bounded openness. When I moved to my current diocese of Durham, I attended a training day for clergy new to the area. The day was about exploring what mission and ministry might look like in this unique part of the world. As part of the day, we watched video clips that showed the daily rhythms of the miners who worked not far from where we sat. The pictures were astonishing and brought home to us just how difficult the conditions were in the mines, and the extent to which these men and boys put their bodies on the line in this work. The footage shifted from the mines to the miners' homes and their families, their communities and streets. It was moving and powerful, and it served its purpose of reminding us of the unique character of the place that is County Durham, and of the numerous places – collieries and mining towns – that were steeped in this work. But at one point in the day one of the new curates to the diocese put her hand up and asked, 'What is it people do now for their living? I mean, the mines closed some time ago: where do people work now?' It was a fascinating moment, because it forced us as a group to reckon with the complexity of this region and of the places within it. That is, we had to ask the question: What is happening now? And how do we make sense of the current situation in light of the history of this place? From this initial question others in the room began to share insights. One curate told us how in her village – a former colliery – the local primary school was having to teach about the history of mining, since the children had no first- or second-hand knowledge of the mines. The point is that to a seventeen-year-old today, Bearpark or Horden, Stanley or Spennymoor are fundamentally different places from those their grandmothers knew at the same age. For many in Durham now, employment looks like commuting to Newcastle, working in one of the region's many call centres or perhaps in the Nissan factory. And all this has brought huge changes to the ways in which families inhabit their places and relate as a community. Some of it is distinctive to this part of the world: the unique reality of being an 'ex'-town (ex-mining/ex-industry) in a northern corner of the country. But much correlates with far wider social and economic trends: increased mobility and individuation, a loss of engagement in local institutions (not just churches), a complexifying of the nature of class and poverty. The challenge then for us in the room (most of whom were parish priests), was to think what it means to be present here, in this place, the County Durham of the 2020s. Such presence would of course have to reckon with the long complex history that is mining; receiving as a gift the deep pride and pain that belongs to that legacy. But simultaneously it must ask what must be done to be Christ here, now, for this generation and for the ones to come.

This experience illustrates what human geographers, like Malpas, mean by place as bounded openness. There are three core components to this tension, each of which are shown in this example. First, place as open means that although places are distinctive and unique, they are always formed by relationship to other places. Second, although places have an identity through time, they are always changing. And third, places can only be fully known from being inside them.

Every place is a relationship of places

First, County Durham is what it is only through a relationship of places, within and without. No place is an island. Former industrial communities like many in County Durham are often the most obvious examples of this. Socio-cultural, economic and political changes happening elsewhere have quite literally defined them. In this sense, 'local' and 'particular' do not go together as neatly as many theological approaches to place assume. The point is that every 'local' place has been uniquely shaped by other places and forces, not least global ones. It would be accurate to say that what makes this place unique is the particular way in which national or global influences have come to play out here, and interact with its existing character. As Massey puts it, 'interdependence and uniqueness [are] two sides of the same coin'.[8] Bounded *and* open. For this reason, we should expect a local place to be unique but we should also expect it to share a great deal with other local places that are like it. Thus, if we want to enter into a place – really get to know it, and dwell there – we must always be thinking within it and beyond it. We might well agree with Davison and Milbank's claim that, 'If the Church is truly to be incarnational, then she must be local', but we need to then ask the vital question: What exactly does it mean to *be* local?[9]

Second, County Durham is what it is only as a collection of places that work together to create the whole. County Durham exists, but so does Thornley and Wynyard, Stockton and Peterlee. This is an important point because the tendency in much theology and defences of the parish has been to equate uniqueness of a place with small scale; that is, the smaller you get, the more unique you become. What makes this account problematic, however, is this assumption about the increasing level of authenticity connected to scale. This was very evident in Nottingham, where I carried out my curacy with a church planting team. What interested me was the way in which the smaller places we ministered within were part of the wider city that is Nottingham. Each place had its own identity – a distinctive story and a character – and yet also shared in the character of the wider city place. There were multiple systems at play, which constituted the wider ecosystem that is Notting-ham. I have come to refer to this as micro and macro place. Micro place is the immediately local: perhaps the street or the neighbourhood, the local shops and so on. But macro place is the place that contains this local place and is made up of potentially multiple micro spaces. The important point is that these macro places are no less authentic than micro places. Structurally, Nottingham functions as a united place, but more importantly people really did see themselves as belong-ing to the city as a whole. The question, What is local? in this context therefore necessitated a complex answer. It is worth noting the differences in the way 'the local' is defined outside the theologies of place I have explored. Nick Clark, for exam-ple, drawing on Peter Taylor, defines locality as: 'the range of ordinary activity, the scale of day-to-day experience and the political-administrative level below the national'.[10] This is a far wider conception of the local than the one that sees local as being that which is (merely) small. Indeed, it is this wider view of the local that inspires movements such as Citizens, which seek to impact across macro spaces (such as a city) through close listening to the needs of citizens in their micro locales. It is interesting to note, for example, that Luke Bretherton, in his important theological work on Citizens, names the movement as a 'local politics'; in opposition to the trends of modernity.[11]

What matters then in defining place is considering how it is experienced by those who are present within it. What are the descriptors used by those in place; where do they see them-selves belonging?

Place is ever-changing

County Durham is continually changing. Many of these changes are unique, but many are local expressions of the global and national trends previously named. As a *bounded* place, Durham has continuity through time, and its history shapes what sort of a place this is. Every year, for example, Durham hosts the annual Miners Gala, an event attended by thousands. However, alongside this continuation of history there are new forces at work, and the place is in flux. We might say that if place is bounded and open, then it is something like a story: there is a past, but there is also a present and a future. There are simply too many examples of the ways that places have changed, and changed quickly, and how new places have emerged. In my own research I spent time in a rural village just south of York, as well as a church in an urban priority area in post-industrial Middlesbrough. Both were wrestling with precisely this phenomenon: how do we be present here when this place has changed, and is changing, so quickly?

This tension between what we value from our local story and the future before us is one we see so often playing out in many of our cultural and political conversations, shaped as they are by the clash of those forces that tend to work for change (progressive; small 'p'), and those that emphasize what is (conservative; small 'c'). It is hard to offer an easy answer to how we hold this tension well. But, clearly, we would want to say that the past must be brought into the present, with care and intentionality. Put simply, good regeneration values what and who is there along with the stories they tell, to bring a richer experience of what was. Bad regeneration ignores the past and gentrifies for financial gain and uninhibited growth.

What is at play, therefore, is the question of how we bring our history into the present. In her book *Dakota: A Spiritual Geography*, Kathleen Norris recounts her experiences of living in a small town in America's Great Plains. In one section, she writes about how the town failed over many years to adequately record, protect and display its social history (public documents, records, artefacts etc.) Norris writes in conclusion that:

> Ironically, it is the town's cherished ideal of changelessness that has helped bring about the devastation, and it is the town's true history that is lost ... [they] may find ... that disconnecting from change does not recapture the past. It loses the future.[12]

It is important that we find new ways to live our history into the present; that is, to bring our history alive. In this sense, it is no good simply saying that we have been present. The question is: What are we to do with this fact now? How can we make this history vital today?

Place can only be known from the inside

'Places', writes Timothy Cresswell, 'are very much things to be inside of.'[13] It is for this reason that much of the writing around place in human geography and other disciplines has turned to the discipline loosely referred to as phenomenology; the exploration of lived human experience. So the argument goes: whatever else place is about it must have to do with what is actually going on for people; not ideas, but how people actually live. In his book, *Life Takes Place*, the geographer David Seamon describes phenomenology as especially interested in the 'unnoticed and taken-for-granted dimensions' of experience.[14] That is, there are ways of being in place that do take lived experience for granted; a sort of assumed presence. One distinction we might make here is between proximity and presence. This is a common issue in the writing around parish; that only by being close ('local') can we be present. My point has been that though they are related, they are not synonymous. To be present one must be proximate to. However, one can be proximate to, and fail to be present. Being present in place requires of us engagement and active attentiveness, and certainly person-to-person encounter. If place is alive (open) rather than simply static (bounded), we cannot be simply there, we must be there intentionally.

Further, when one does engage fully in place it becomes clear just how contested place is. The Killers' 2021 album, *Pressure Machine*, is something of a concept album – it explores life in a small, ex-industrial town, in the USA. The album begins with an audio recording, which presents a stark dissonance in the experience of life in this place. We hear from one female resident who tells us in 'homely' tones that she's grown up in the town, found a partner here and feels settled. The tape then clicks forward, and we hear the account of a violent assault in this same town, from a man who delivers his story in an intentionally matter-of-fact manner. Before his story can be finished the tape clicks back to the initial recording, where we hear again from the woman who tells us that she'll be in this – her home town – for ever. The recordings are set side by side like this to make the point: a stark reminder that perceptions of place differ radically depending on one's experience of it. Same space, very different senses of place. Human geographers have wanted to make some sense of all this; how it can be that a place can be viewed entirely differently from different people and groups within it. This itself is an important realization for a church claiming to be the national church, and an awareness of our own history must immediately make us sceptical of grand claims to faithful presence. We know that the church was often complicit in the erosion of people's places; often on the wrong side of the power imbalances that marked many local communities. We may have been implicated in real places, but because place is a debate about meaning and identity through competing narratives, such proximity could never be neutral, and we may well question the choices the church made in siding with certain such narratives.

It is often the case that the complexity we see as central to place is presented as monolithic. For example, an ex-mining village is shown to be complex because of the economic deprivation of that place and all that results. Complexity here means financial poverty, and perhaps a lack of aspiration. However, this is just one story at work in that place. There are other stories and other forces at play that are just as integral. The role of immigration, the new call-centre economy, increased technological access and so on. To pick up Oliver O'Donovan's argument about the loss of a sense of place, we might well agree with him but also push the point that there is never only one sense of a place, but multiple 'senses'.

So we can see what it might mean to speak of place as bounded and open. Place is a tension between the settled nature of its identity, and the fact that: every place exists as and in a relationship of places; places change and new places emerge; place is not easily definable from the outside, but consists of multiple (often competing) stories that can only be fully known from within. This complexifies the four colours of place that I outlined in Chapter 1. Place is particular; not by being discrete, but as a unique coming together of other places and existing as a relationship of places. Place embraces complexity, but in the fullest sense, recognizing the competition of narratives about the identity of each place, and the fact that such complexity can only be fully known from within. Place is about a connection to the past, but is not regressive; there is no one simple account of a place's history, and its past is always becoming. And place offers permanence, but not eternally so. Place changes – sometimes drastically – and new places are continually emerging.

Segue: a theology of bounded openness through the Good Samaritan

I have argued that theology's shift to take place seriously has tended to overemphasize one side of the tension inherent in place, namely that place is bounded. What then of place as both bounded *and* open? Place as both unique and yet interdependent, settled and yet changing, observable from the outside and yet only understood from the inside? Does this make sense theologically? I think so, and I think such a theology is vital for the church as it wrestles with how we are to be truly present in our places. To explore this, I turn to the parable of the Good Samaritan, which comes to us in Luke 10. The purpose of Jesus' parables is to invite engagement with meaning, and this one is no different: I am aware of the range of (sometimes competing) interpretations that the narrative makes possible.[15] However, I want to use this parable as a sort of narrative holder for the wider theological vision that I see as integral to scripture's witness, as well as to the Christian tradition. That is, I believe we see here scripture's way of holding both the bounded and the open in tension.

First then, place as bounded. One of the striking things about this parable is that it is set in a named location: 'down [the road] from Jerusalem to Jericho'. We only have one other parable where Jesus does this.[16] And the characters too are 'placed'. The man is loved as a Jewish man, and the man loves as a Samaritan. Their places of origin matter. Indeed, they are the basis of the radical redefining of neighbourliness that is the parable's heart. One cannot redefine what is not real, and as has been argued by many interpreters of this parable, Jesus is not offering a universal ethic – 'everyone must love everyone' – rather he grounds the story in the particularities of the relationship of Jews and Samaritans in particular places (Jerusalem and Jericho). Jesus is not saying to love everyone the same, but to love each in the way you are, and the way they are (and we might add: to love everyone *from* where you and they are). We have here the parabolic version of O'Donovan's point that to love everyone is to love no one.

The parable, therefore, shows us how bounded place is what makes possible *real* love. The Samaritan refuses to see this other as example of a type ('just another Jew') but receives him, as it were, as gift. The error made by those who walk past is that they do the opposite, seeing here not a beloved individual but a type of thing, be that 'victim', 'a wounded man' or 'a problem/threat'. This argument about valuing people, as we saw in Chapter 1, has been critical to defences of place.

The Samaritan man is the embodiment of Ben Quash's idea of 'finding': when we simply show up in existing places, and listen hard, we find the beginnings of at least the possibility that we will encounter people as they truly are.

And yet there is more going on in this passage; ways in which Jesus disrupts our settled understandings of place. In this sense it also shows place in its 'openness'. The first thing to say is that this passage is a prophetic performance. As has been pointed out by good preachers through time, Jesus is intentional about making the Jewish man the survivor here, rather than the saviour. The story thus serves to shatter established categories, even the categories that Jesus' listeners (that is, Jewish women and men) may have assumed in good faith to be valid responses to his teaching. He refuses them the easy conclusion, 'We should love everyone, even our enemies.' No, says Jesus, the first step is to recognize yourself as the one in need. You cannot possibly hope to help others so long as you think you are in the position of strength. Thus, this parable is not in the first instance counter-cultural but counter-ethical; Jesus calls us to a new posture and nothing less than a new heart. There are established norms, even established hopeful expectations, and then there is the new and deeper work that God is doing. What God has gifted, God may take away to bring you into even greater gift. Where a place has been settled and bounded for some time as a gift of God, God is not bound to it indefinitely. God is at work in both the constancy and in the flux.

Another way of looking at this is to say that what we see in this passage is the interaction of both place *and* time. Time is mentioned explicitly in verse 35 ('The next day...') but I mean more than this. Time in the sense of things happening. It's an obvious thing to say, but in this parable, things happen! And the important point is that as things happen, the places themselves change. The road becomes something new through the course of the parable: from a journeying place; now to a place marked by violence; then to a place of courageous and sacrificial love. Then the scene switches to another place, to which we are (with the wounded man) carried in love. There is a small – though I think significant – detail in verse 32 when Luke uses the Greek word *topos*, one of the two Greek terms for place. Thus: 'a Levite, when he came to the place and saw him'. In this journey between two places, we have now a new place. Before, this was simply terrain – a road; now, because of this event, it has become a place.

We might call this the way in which place is always becoming. Places emerge, places change. This 'becoming' nature of place is very important in the human geography literature, and is integral to Malpas' definition of place as 'bounded openness'. Massey defined her own work as an attempt to reconcile what she saw as the restrictive divide between space and time in our thinking. For her, what matters is 'space-time'; the way place is about boundaries *and* about change. New places emerge, old places disappear, existing places undergo significant change. It is significant then that both Andrew Rumsey and John Inge land their reflections on place in eschatology; that the new creation relativizes all places. No place is permanent, and our commitment to place cannot be the most significant one, because God promises to break in anew.[17] In theological terms we would want to say that place is a becoming because God is always becoming. This is why Rowan Williams has been critical of the idea of the 'sacramental principle' that can often be found lurking behind defences of place in theology. Such an idea, Williams argues, negates God's activity, supposing that the world is already suffused with divine presence. For Williams, it is important that we say God becomes present again and again.[18] It is this theology, which emphasizes God's initiating freedom, that has been at the heart of this book. As I argued in Chapter 2, it is what makes possible our being committed to what we have received without being bound to it. The same underlying principle is at play here. Place is a given reality, but it is not so for all time. This nature of place as becoming because God is always becoming is – I think – the richest way we have of speaking theologically of place, since it seems to me to make sense of the tensions inherent in scripture and within the Christian tradition.

What we see in the parable is, I have suggested, the complex and often confusing way in which place is encountered in the Bible and Christian tradition. Bounded place is important; Jesus does not override given places with a universalizing (we could say, 'modern') ethic. And yet, at the same time, he shows how the work of God is to engage in new ways with the flux of place, even causing new places to emerge. This is precisely what we see through scripture. Thus, in the Bible, alongside the 'settled' dimension of life with God (the constant placed encounters with God, from the burning bush to Bethel; the gift of the land and the rootedness of God's people; the incarnation; the first churches and their epistles being named according to their location; the eschatological vision of a new city place) there is also the 'unsettled': the motif of wilderness and exile, the kingdom of God as transcending the borders of Israel, the warnings against tribal identity as final. Yes, place is vital, but God is not bound to it, and can pull us out of it. He can create new places, and he frequently encounters his people in – yes – a place, but a strange place, one they would never have expected. The God of the scriptures sends out as much as settles. It is this that lies behind Jesus' warnings about family loyalty, and his call to reject the received bounds of one's birthplace or tribe.[19] It is also this that defines the character of Jesus' own ministry, which is so obviously marked more by movement than by fixity. This dimension of the scriptural witness we can name as the 'apocalyptic'. The apocalyptic is about unsettling; into the settled order of things comes a new and different reality, the rule, or kingdom, of God. In other words, the God of the Bible both affirms what is, and does a new thing. In our terms, God gifts us place, and values places, but is not bound to them.

This then is the fundamental tension at the heart of all Christian tradition: between Good Friday and Easter Sunday, cross and resurrection, Jesus' ascension and his coming again. The now and the not yet. Christianity in its first few centuries found itself in a strange place of affirming the created order as it is (and thus, places as they are), since it was created by the good creator God, but also wanting to say that the same God was up to something radically new in Jesus and through the power of the Spirit. Gnosticism really was a temptation for the early church. My point is that the church's rejection of this option was not a rejection of radical newness in favour of static physical givens, but was a courageous, and astonishing, embrace of the tension. God takes on flesh and thus affirms our humanity. But in doing so he transforms it. In this way Christianity has always wanted to affirm both what was and what is, and pray in anticipation for what is to come. Put simply, Christians will be those looking back and looking forwards at the same time; they will want to affirm the 'natural' stories of each place, as they are, but will always be open to the possibility that God can and will do a new thing here. It will not be a surprise to Christians that places remain and that places change, for this makes sense of the God revealed in Jesus Christ. In Chapter 1, I mentioned how significant the Benedictine Rule is to Quash's defence of place. And this is right. However, alongside the Benedictine tradition we have others, for example the Franciscan, with its emphasis on movement and wandering. The existence of these two traditions speaks of this tension perfectly. Staying and going. Place and time. Constancy and change. Rootedness and roaming. Both are faithful witnesses to God's activity in the world.

James Jennings argues that a Christian doctrine of creation is 'a way of seeing place in its fullest sense'.[20] My argument has been that this fullest sense of place includes both place's boundaries and constancy, as well as its change. Jennings too points us in this direction, more aware than any other recent theologian of the way place is contested, manipulated and open to being used as a tool of suppression. Place is always becoming. To be faithful here – present in place – will necessitate our being responsive and creative. We cannot work against placelessness by a reassertion of boundaries and structure alone. Ultimately the tensions highlighted by human geographers resonate with the fundamental tensions at the heart of the Christian faith, encapsulated in the fact of God's continual giving. The language of bounded openness should not surprise us as Christians since we live in the now and the not yet; looking backwards and forwards. It is to this forward vision for the parish that I turn next. Avoiding nostalgia, can parish be reclaimed in our time?

Notes

1 Edward Casey, quoted in Ingrid Leman Stefanovic, 2000, *Safeguarding our Common Future: Rethinking Sustainable Development*, New York: State University of New York Press, p. 116.

2 According to the authors of the *Dictionary of Human Geography*, human geographers in the last few decades can be understood to have overcome three sets of 'oppositions': time and space; absolute and relative space; and abstract and concrete space. Each of these in a sense is about the relationship of space and place. See 2000, 'Space', in *The Dictionary of Human Geography*, R. J. Johnson et al. (eds), 4th edn, London: Blackwell, p. 771.

3 Martin Robinson, 2020, *The Place of the Parish: Imagining Mission in our Neighbourhood*, London: SCM Press.

4 Doreen Massey, 1991, 'A Global Sense of Place', at http://aughty.org/pdf/global_sense_place.pdf, accessed 02.03.2021.

5 Jeff Malpas, 'Thinking Topographically: Space, Place and Geography', *Il Cannocchiale: Rivista di studi filosofici*, 42:1–2 (2001), pp. 25–53.

6 Malpas, 'Thinking Topographically'.

7 Malpas, 'Putting Space in Place: Philosophical Topography and Relational Geography', *Planning and Environment D: Society and Space*, 30:2 (2012), pp. 226–42.

8 Doreen Massey, 'Questions of Locality', *Geography*, 78:2 (1993), pp. 142–9, 145.

9 Andrew Davison and Alison Milbank, 2010, *For the Parish: A Critique of Fresh Expressions*, London: SCM Press, p. 154.

10 Nick Clarke, 'Locality and Localism: A View from British Human Geography', *Policy Studies*, 34:5–6 (2013), pp. 492–507.

11 Luke Bretherton, 2010, *Christianity and Contemporary Politics: The Conditions and Possibilities of Faithful Witness*, London: Wiley-Blackwell, p. 105.

12 Kathleen Norris, 1993, *Dakota: A Spiritual Geography*, New York: Houghton Mifflin, p. 64.

13 Tim Cresswell, 2004, *Place: A Short Introduction*, Oxford: Blackwell, p. 28.

14 David Seamon, 2018, *Life Takes Place: Phenomenology, Life-worlds, and Place Making*, London: Routledge.

15 See Nick Spencer, 2017, *The Political Samaritan: How Power Hijacked a Parable*, London: Bloomsbury.

16 Luke 18.9–14 (at the temple). There is debate whether 'the sea' in Matthew 13.47–50 is necessarily the Sea of Galilee.

17 John Inge, 2003, *A Christian Theology of Place*, Aldershot: Ashgate, pp. 138f.; Andrew Rumsey, 2017, *Parish: An Anglican Theology of Place*, London: SCM Press, pp. 170f.

18 See Rowan Williams, 2000, *On Christian Theology*, London: Blackwell, pp. 197ff.

19 For example, Matthew 8.22 and Luke 9.60.

20 Willie James Jennings, 2010, *The Christian Imagination: Theology and the Origins of Race*, New Haven, CT: Yale University Press, p. 248.

4

Putting the Parish in its Place

This book has been an attempt to pull the language of parish away from the parish structure. I said in Chapter 2 that this is not about rejecting structure per se. Rather the task is to assess our current structures and ask whether and how they are allowing the vocation to presence, which resonates with good theological instincts about place, to happen. In this chapter I want to pursue that task in light of the nature of place itself. If place is always a relationship of places, and is ever changing, what does this mean for our vocation to be present here? As part of this I want to think through the question of new churches and the language of the mixed ecology, exploring why and how new churches might be part of the church's commitment to be present. The starting point is to fathom what being 'present in place' might actually mean. We can then ask how this task relates to the current parish structure: the lines on a map, the buildings across the landscape and parochial resourcing at deanery, diocesan and national levels. If place can only be known from the inside, we must be very clear about what it is we think that the structures and systems – imposed as they are from the 'outside' – are doing.

The problem with coverage: imagined presence and intentionality

There is a scene in the film *Billy Elliot* that brilliantly captures the importance of knowing a place from within. Billy has travelled from his home in County Durham for an audition at the

Royal School of Ballet in London. In the changing room, one of the other boys (in perfect received pronunciation) takes the initiative to speak to Billy. 'Where are you from?' the boy asks. 'Everington. County Durham', Billy replies. The boy looks pleased; he has been trained in the art of conversation and has found his 'in'. 'Durham. Isn't there an amazing cathedral?' And Billy's reply reveals all we might need to know about the phenomenon that is place. 'I don't know,' says Billy, 'I've never been.'

The scene is a helpful check on what I shall call here an imagined presence. Looking at Durham from a distance, everything in us wants to say that Durham Cathedral must be integral to the place and the people of this region. We could bring to mind the postcards that show the cathedral, its visibility in the heart of the city or its role in significant annual events through the year. And from all this we might conclude that the cathedral is therefore significant for all, and not least for families such as Billy's. I have heard many a church person in Durham articulate something like this. What Billy's reaction reveals, however, is that we cannot assume that the cathedral holds that sort of a place. For so many who call this part of the world home, the cathedral, whether we like it or not, simply is not all that significant to their lives. Not as a historical site, and certainly not as a spiritual or religious one. Despite being in the same region, and despite being used elsewhere as a public symbol for their region, the fact is that their place is not the cathedral's place.

The example from *Billy Elliot* shines a light on what I think are two dangers when we think about our presence as a national church. The first is an imagined coverage, and the second is an imagined presence. The former relates most of all to our national and diocesan decision-making, and the latter more to those on the ground, in the churches.

First then, imagined coverage. The Church of England is able to make a claim that other denominations are not in a position to make. 'A Christian Presence in every Community' is aspirational as much as it is a statement of fact. However, there is just enough around us to allow us to think that it might be getting there. Specifically, we have maps and we have churches. Both serve as a sort of physical embodiment of an assumed coverage and thus allow the imaginary of our presence in every place to persevere. That word 'imaginary' is important. The process of 'mapping' a terrain has been a fascination for many in the field of human geography and beyond – how reality can be shaped from distance, and the impact this has on the one doing the mapping as well as on the recipients of the map. A map forms our imaginary. Because we can see the lines and because we can list the buildings, we come to believe that we are therefore implicated here, involved and engaged. To be clear, I am not questioning the principle of coverage, and especially not the task of mapping. I think it is spiritually significant, and it is one part of what it means for us to receive the vocation for the cure of souls of all. Essentially it matters that we can see areas for which we have a responsibility to pray; to be able to say that every community in the country is prayed for. But saying that the church has every area mapped, and churches scattered across the landscape, is fundamentally different from making a claim about our presence. And imaginaries do matter; our perceptions of reality shape our decision-making. What I have in mind here is the possibility that, if we believe we have the place covered by virtue of the lines and the lists, then the aim of the game becomes resourcing this structure. An imperceptible shift occurs, where we no longer ask how we become present here but rather: How do we sustain this system? In this sense, coverage works well as means, but less well as an end. As the environmental geographer Ingrid Stefanovic argues, 'Genuine dwelling can remain close only if it avoids the closure of total-izing visions.'[1] Our work is to ensure that the parish structure and all that sustains does not become for us such a vision.

Alongside an imagined coverage we have imagined presence on the ground, in our churches. It is possible, and we know this, to believe that one is vital in one's place, but miss the reality. The presence of a building is often a part of this. We feel close to where people are, we pray for them, but in fact we are not connected. Again, this is not to deny the importance of prayer and sacrament; we have to say that the first job of the church is to hold its people in prayer. If our communities don't know we are there for them, we must remain convinced that God is there with them and that he hears our prayers. However, my sense of spending time with the four churches during my research was that the longing to be known and to know really did matter. And it mattered because of love: love draws us out of ourselves towards the other, so that those for whom we pray we also long to meet and to share life with.

This longing is therefore the best way to get to a definition of what it is I mean by being present in place. The concept is hard to pin down but is, I think, whatever it is we are longing for as we love our places. It is thus a description of genuine interaction between the good news of Christ with the people and communities around us; a real meeting of these things. It is full – missional in the broadest sense – and will of course take on different flavours given the theological instincts of the church and its congregation. Again, it is about more than church growth, measured as it were in terms of the contribution to the common good. My point is that presence in place must involve a sense of reciprocation; not just what is offered but also what is received, heard, felt and known. It is therefore about social capital: a church is present in place to the extent it has real capital in its place. If it is not this, then the concept of presence in place quickly loses any substantive meaning. Do the people and communities of this place know we are there? Do they know that we pray? Of course, in some instances this presence will be hard going, and it might be that there will be little reception of our commitment to be in place. The capital is less. This does not negate the definition but affirms it. That our love for place is not received as we would want is not the issue. What matters is that there is a seeking after connection between church and her place. Again, presence in place is a becoming rather than an achievable target. The point is that we must not mistake proximity for presence.

We sometimes need to hear the voices of our sisters and

brothers in other churches to become aware of the fact of imagined coverage and imagined presence. Our claim to coverage is often felt not only as somewhat arrogant, but also blind to reality. I hear this a great deal from my friends in majority black churches. What they would point out is that the Church of England, for example, was not and has not been good at being present in places of high ethnic diversity and immigration. The accusation of systemic racism in the Church of England thus needs some complexifying. We must be attuned to the *way* in which such attitudes played out and especially how they were written into our engagement with place. We were not present in the places of immigration and ethnic diversity. If you like, we had these places covered, but we were not present there. Thus, when the moment came, we were not present to respond – to welcome, to love. Parochial ministry was static when it should have been dynamic. We can only expect to see a church as diverse as the places it sits within – and certainly a church leadership as such – if we are genuinely present where we have up to now been only spatially so.

Intentional presence

Presence in place is therefore an active task that is concerned first and foremost with the ministry of engagement in that place. In this sense, parish is an act. There is no shortcut or bypass to this, and we have to be aware of how conversations about structure can be the very thing preventing us taking this task seriously.

The language I use for this with my students is the language of intentionality. I like the word 'intentional' when speaking of Christian vocation because it implies deliberation and decision, without the baggage of intended outcomes. I think we can say that in the New Testament, whether we look at Jesus in the Gospels or Paul as examples, mission is intentional but not outcomes-driven. We intentionally step out upon the water in faith, not exactly sure what the result might be. The central takeaway from my research with four churches was that presence in place is an intentional step. Some churches had been intentional and were present, others had not and were not.

This fact of intentionality is one of the reasons why I find myself disagreeing with the idealized version of the parish presented in the likes of *For the Parish* or John Milbank's 'Stale Expressions'. To state again, I find myself in a strange position reading these: in agreement with the premises but so at odds with the conclusions. Take, for example the issue of diversity that I highlighted above. The consensus in the literature is that the church is called to model unity in diversity in a world that does the opposite. And it is the parish that is held to do this. In Milbank's words, 'Only pure geography encompasses all without exception.'[2] But, of course, he is only at best half right. Geography cannot embrace *anybody*. A church rooted in its place, present there, might well do so. I think of one of the churches I researched, which had actively welcomed Iranian refugees: working with the local council to establish where areas of resettlement were, putting up signs in the church in Farsi, encouraging those refugees with musical skill to join the worship group. The point is that the diversity sought by the likes of Milbank is not the work of the parish, but the hard prayerful work of close presence in place. It takes intentionality because so often we are working against the grain, not only of the places we sit within, but of the very culture of our churches themselves.

Intentional presence in place therefore happens at the church and congregational level. As well as writing of global and supranational spatial realities, human geographers give a great deal of time to the small acts of place-building at local levels. We should therefore get better at telling stories of how churches are taking that step of owning the parish vocation and becoming intentionally present. In my research I noted how churches were doing this well. Above all, I saw that churches deeply rooted in place knew their places and the people within them well. They recognized that there is a real problem if advertisers know the tendencies of the people of their place better than they do.

Instead, they seek to listen hard, understand and learn from other similar places. I saw the importance of leadership; of the lay or ordained person who sought to drive the whole people of Christ in that place towards greater engagement. I saw the importance of fostering what I called a 'parochial imaginary' in the church: recognizing that the fact of the parish boundary and the vocation of the cure of souls needed to be brought to life and made real. This meant preaching and teaching about it; speaking of the local place and celebrating presence constantly. Local leaders would find new language to articulate this calling, so that others could participate in it. All of this served to build a parish community who loved their place.

Presence and subsidiarity

My argument thus far has been that presence can only be earned and not assumed. Just as a failure to be attentive in a parish can lead to a loss of connection between the church and the people for a generation, so too a failure to be implicated in the real places of the nation – to be vital in place – leaves that vocation to national presence thin. In this sense, the national vocation is built from the bottom up, as it were. It consists not of the maps or the fact of the churches, and not in the diocesan structures, but in the day-to-day transformative ministry of presence in place.

If we begin with that idea that place can only be known in the act of engagement – on the ground – then everything else is relativized accordingly. In other words, the questions about our structures, systems, training and resourcing need to be: How does this (aspect) lead to increased presence in place? One way of framing this is through the principle of subsidiarity, which has been central within Roman Catholic social teaching and is beginning to pop up elsewhere.[3] Subsidiarity is about 'feasibility' of structure, and its claim is that decisions should be taken at the 'lowest practicable' level.[4] In this sense, subsidiarity is really about locality and scale. However, I want to stretch the idea to suggest that it might be a helpful way of thinking about the church's vocation to be present. If, as I am arguing, the church is present only by being in real place, implicated on the ground, then this must be the goal and strategic priority of the church's structures and the direction towards which all else should flow. According to the principle of subsidiarity, therefore, every action but also every structure must be measured by the extent to which it is working towards this end and enabling that presence to occur.

Take as an example the number of mission and ministry roles within a diocese, a target of frequent derision by some within the Save the Parish movement ('Managerialism!'). The claim, of course, is that out of the limited pot that is a diocese's budget, such posts inevitably draw away from front-line ministry. It is impossible to make a blanket conclusion about all of this here. However, if we take the principle of subsidiarity and presence in place, then we begin to find some grounds to evaluate these roles. It might be that within a diocese they serve as part of the 'fictionalizing' of place that I identified above. We appoint people at the diocesan level because it can make us feel that we are achieving something at the local level, just in the same way that reinforcing the parish structure convinces us that we have coverage. Presence – in mission, evangelism, work with older people or young people and so on – cannot be done from distance. However, the principle of subsidiarity asks the secondary question: What structures or personnel are required to enable this local presence to happen? It acknowledges that because of the nature of place there must be joined-up and strategic thinking when it comes to being present, which enables the local resources to be deployed and equipped well. One thinks of youth facilitators or those working to support churches tackle food poverty. In this instance, the role, far from inhibiting presence in place, may well be a vital tool in allowing it to happen.

There are many similar issues where we might think more creatively about the relationship between the immediate ministry of presence, and extra-parochial strategies and tools. At the micro level of a parish, it is very difficult to sustain a youth group or a ministry to young professionals or a support network for recovering addicts. But such things can be established by and with a number of parishes. The question again is: Is this thing helping the church and the churches be more present to the people and their places? A shared youth programme across a number of parishes is not anti-parish in this sense, but is enabling that local presence to happen. The point, again, is that the direction – towards greater presence – is a check on the value of such programmes and projects.

Training

Finally, if presence in place is a result of intentionality then there is an onus on us to think about what it is we believe we are training people for, especially those called to ordination in the threefold order. If I am right, that parochial ministry is a pioneering task – that presence is earned – then we do have to train people accordingly. As I hope has been clear thus far, I am not here attempting to drive a wedge between good pastoral practice and intentional or strategic mission (I hope the error made by the distinction between 'pastoral' and 'missional' should be obvious by this point; it lets inherited parochial ministry off the hook in terms of mission while also implying that mission could *be* mission without presence and service). However, it does mean that we need to help those who feel a call to be deacons or priests in place, to work out how they might bridge that gap between church and place. How they might find often very simple ways to connect the life of the church with the life of the community. It is not a shift in theology, so much as in mindset and skillset. This is why that word 'intentional' is important. We should all be intentional in connecting our praxis (whatever shade of tradition that praxis might represent) with those who are yet to know of it. Sadly, 'mission' has somehow become mixed up with 'evangelical', and this is a great loss to the whole.

I hope so far to have given some insight about the form that our commitment to place might take. I have argued that what matters most is a genuine presence in which the churches, and therefore the church, is vital, implicated in its place. Indeed, this resonates with one of the central conclusions in the conversation about place in our time: that place is about what is real and tangible, in contrast to the fictions of space. Imagined presence and imagined coverage are 'spatial' in this sense: projecting on to what is, a story of our own making. To be present in place, however, demands immediacy and intentionality. We must really be there, engaged and involved. I want now to consider how we might think about this task given the two other aspects of place, as bounded and open, explored in the previous chapter. Thus, how might we be present in place given that place is a connection of places, and is ever-changing?

Place as an interconnection of places

I argued in the previous chapter that one of the marks of place as bounded openness is that place exists through a relationship of other places. I used there the language of micro and macro place and suggested that we see both as places in the fullest sense. The important question to ask is: Where do the people of this locale define their place of belonging? It should not be controversial to note that most (though, as I find in my research, definitely not all) people in the country do not see themselves as belonging to our parish spaces. In some cases this is because the parish is too big (they see themselves as belonging to a micro space, e.g. an estate) and in other cases the parish is too small (people see themselves belonging to a macro place, e.g. a city). My argument is that we should seek to be present to the places people use as their identifiers. This is important because it is places rather than spaces that can be objects of love. That is, the lines on the map – as abstract space – cannot motivate us through desire for the other. We love not a space, but a place: a particular street, row of shops, neighbourhood or city. So it is important that in our parochial imaginary we are bound less to the lines and more to the places themselves. A number of points follow on from this.

The relationship between the big and the small has always been a challenge for the parochial system, with its focus on small, discrete units and over-representation in rural places,[5] and there is much that we can learn from this history. For example, the rate of population growth due to urbanization following industrialization quickly stretched a system that had relied on there being one official parish church for an urban district. In Liverpool, for example, which was considered to come under the remit of one rectory, the population grew from 10,000 in 1700 to almost 150,000 by 1831.[6] Though the church's response in each city differed, common reactions were to restructure dioceses, build new churches and create new parish boundaries or districts.[7] Even when new churches were built and boundaries created, however, the question remained as to whether the principle of parish and parochial responsibility could really work. For instance, the drawing of boundaries was seen to be far more complex in urban settings, where there were less defined centres of culture and economy. Furthermore, it was felt by some that the rapid building of churches and creation of parishes micronized the system, with too many parishes sitting alongside one another. This had the unintended impact of stretching resources – as churches and rectories needed to be manned – but also tended towards a parochialism rather than a combined, strategic ministry.[8]

Whether the same conclusions apply today is not my concern. What I want to observe is the thinking behind the argument levelled against the way the structure was handled at the time: that because place is a multitude of micro and macro, we need to think hard about how we respond to place in its interconnectedness. I do not think we can make a blanket statement that the parish does not work well in urban contexts. However, it is the case that being present to a city will entail something more than subdividing responsibility on the basis of geographical units. Issues such as food poverty, homelessness or the manipulation of a vulnerable low-paid workforce demand joined-up thinking. As has been said many times before, we need to be better at this if we are to prevent the parish becoming a parochialism. To return to the earlier theme, it seems to me that one of the things preventing such reimagining of the parish is a commitment to the structure, or to the ideal of coverage dispersed across parishes with bounded areas of responsibility. If that is the case, then it is the structure itself that is working against the vocation.

In an ideal world it would be the deanery, held in the Chapter, that would enable a healthy balance between micro and macro, and especially across macro places such as the cities. My experience suggests that this is not happening very frequently. Again, the idea of intentionality is important. It will not be the existence of a deanery or event of a Chapter meeting that will enable shared ministry to happen, it will only happen through intentional creating and building of relationships; a genuine collegiality in shared purpose. (Indeed, as well as often functioning poorly, the deanery Chapter is hamstrung by the fact that it is not a decision-making body.) What is required, therefore, is a space at the macro-local level in which a conversation can be had, and decisions made, about how resources are shared and especially how existing buildings are used. What I want to establish here is at least the possibility that reordering ministry like this might be done in such a way that it enables the church to be more rooted in place than less. That, say, the closure of a smaller church congregation in one part of the city may not necessarily be a sign of a church pulling away from its responsibility to its local place, but part of a shared vision across the parishes towards more sustained presence. As has been said elsewhere, the hope is not to close church buildings permanently or to sell them (especially not to seek quick financial wins), but to close them for a season in order to focus on the work of becoming present across the macro place, and in the hope that one day the building will become again a home for the fruit of such presence.

This said, I do think Andrew Rumsey is right to name the

fundamental danger with the attempt to shift away from parish towards other macro forms of distributing ministry, such as mission areas or minster regions.[9] Rumsey notes that the problem with such initiatives is that they meet 'the soulless task of attempting to introduce new forms of place that are devoid of any cultural meaning'.[10] I think he is right, which is why the important thing is to work out where places are and seek locality there. Our ministry must be located in real places, the places people outside the church identify, name and feel a sense of belonging to, rather than a fictional place that we have mapped from a distance. Again, such places may be micro and they may be macro.

What excites me, therefore, is not the merging of parishes or the enlarging of benefices, but rather systems that allow multiple parishes to work collegiately across a certain macro space, while maintaining their distinctive presence in their respective micro place. I think of several examples of where this is happening well. These local 'nets' or 'families' of churches work as a collection of parish churches – with their area of responsibility – and pioneer projects across a geographical area. They have come about through directed financial investment, which has provided for growing teams of clergy (curates, incumbents) and lay workers (youth workers, operations and admin support). These projects recognize the importance of leadership in each (parish) place. In some cases, the collection of churches consists of some churches that were close to closure but are now seeing regular worship and service to their locales. What makes the system work in each instance is the sense of a shared vision and resourcing at this local level. Lay and ordained leaders are rooted in their parishes and lead the parish church, but they gather as a team to pray and support one another. Larger, better-resourced churches naturally help the lesser-resourced communities. There is a shared admin hub as well as safeguarding support so that no one church carries the weight of this alone. Because these are micro places in one macro place, there are similar issues faced in each place, and thus the team share wisdom, and problem-solve together. In terms of the legal structures, arrangements such as JCCs (joint church councils) have helped concretize otherwise informal arrangements. The best of these projects have worked organically, rejecting any notion of empire-building or of a strategy to 'take over' parishes. Expressions of tradition and worship styles have been valued. One leader of a network of churches told me in very clear terms that he believed church in urban places like his must be small and placed rather than big and attractional. His language was that of a net; 'The resource', he said, 'is the net.' If we take this idea forward, the claim is that we do need to think strategically about resources, but this cannot be achieved through investing in one or two large churches. Rather it is the network, the sharing of vision and training and skills that enables these very local expressions. I think these examples demonstrate what is possible when we deploy resources wisely to prioritize local churches within a macro space through a collegial approach. The point is that the structure is reimagined to enable intentional presence to happen.

Place as ever-changing

The nature of place is that it changes. One way we can be sure we are not moving towards presence in place, therefore, is by being inflexible to change. There has been a wariness in many parts of the church to speak of being responsive to change, since to do so would seem to play precisely into the instrumentalist way of thinking inherent to modernity. *Mission-shaped Church*, for example, made the now frequently noted observation that in our time people are less rooted geographically and tend to associate on other grounds, such as through networks or interest groups, the assumption being that our churches should therefore reflect this fact. In response to such claims, the arguments about the church's difference, which I observed in Chapter 1, came to the fore. The danger, so it was argued, was that for the sake of missional impact we respond in an unthinking way, establishing church in whatever form so long as it works. (We will have different conceptions of what 'working' looks like based on our ecclesial instincts, but probably something such as numerical growth or local impact and so on) Thus, we plant non-parish churches or form church based around interest groups or whatever it might be.

There is more that must be said about this than I could possibly hope to offer here. However, in line with the argument of this book I think we would want to question some of the thinking around how people relate to place in our time. The immediate question to ask is whether the kind of human life envisaged by *Mission-shaped Church* is really what we believe to be the best form of human life. The argument of this book has been that if place matters to what it is to be human as God created and restored us, then we should be aware of the cultural trends that seek to dislocate us from place. What I did find in my research is that people in churches were drawn – fresh expressions or not – to local place and local commitment, and I am thus sceptical that any genuinely 'displaced' church is ever possible. I return below to the question of new churches and how they might relate (or not) to places. I do, however, think that we will need to do better in many of our churches at challenging some of these trends we imbibe so easily. The 'addiction to destination' may well need to be named and challenged in some of our places. This itself, however, is a further example of where the challenge to modernity comes, not through a commitment to structure as much as a commitment to discipleship, and what Rumsey calls 'place formation'. Parish might become the ground upon which people learn how to be local and love place, but it will become so only intentionally, and our inherited parish churches are no less susceptible to consumerism or post-institutionalism than any other church. One final observation to make on this is that I thought at the time, and still do now, that the conclusions about place in *Mission-shaped Church* had a certain 'suburban' flavour; in the same way that it has been the rural imaginary that has tended to define the defences of the parish. In both instances, the missiological reflection has inclined to be shaped by the types of people who do attend churches rather than the very many who don't. Clearly, many people in our nation are more transient and live more 'fluid' lives than ever. But many don't. If 'presence in place' is to come alive for the Church of England, my sense is that it will indeed find its revival in the estates, the industrial towns and forgotten places of the nation.

A few further comments about how the church responds to place as ever-changing will suffice at this point.

First, it is only by being close to the ground – present in places – that the consequences of modernity's assault on place can be truly known. It has been humbling, for example, to observe the role that the churches played and have continued to play following the tragedy at Grenfell in 2017. On the multiple issues that our eyes were so violently opened to on that day the Church of England has been able to be in several conversations at once: at the centre and in the local. Thus, it matters that the local church was there, in place, so as to highlight not simply the immediate tragedy (which was all too obvious), but the far deeper, insidious tragedy, so much of which could be defined as a devaluing of people's lived place. Likewise, it is worth noting the Archbishops' Council 2021 report on housing, *Coming Home*. The report speaks of good homes as good places and makes important observations about the way in which our society frequently downplays this, offering instead homes that are functional, based on vapid economic principles. What the report and its reception demonstrates is that the Church of England still has something important to say in the public sphere about the nature of place and locality; contribution that has validity because of the church's commitment to the immediacy of communities in place. Unless we are rooted in place we lose the ability to critique cultural trends, because we fail to see their human impact.

Second, there are many ways in which places change and emerge that are not a result of a deliberate process of place erosion. Places simply change. Our structures and systems must be able to respond to such changes at every level if our presence is to mean anything at all. The challenge is that change is perpetual and continual. Thus, responsiveness is not a one-off activity, as though we could take stock every decade and revaluate our place commitment. Rather responsiveness is a frame of mind, and a habit which must be built into the system. A housing estate expands, a rural village becomes a commuter district, a new transport hub is built nearby. In situations like this, one answer might well be to redraw parish boundaries. I have little doubt that in some situations this will indeed be the right answer, and we need to be able to do this quickly and well. But in this instance, the far more pressing issue seems to be about both permission and cooperation that refuse parochialism, and a simultaneous redistribution of resources. The question again to ask is whether our priority is maintaining the structure – the sense of coverage and imagined presence – or enabling genuine presence in place.

New churches and the mixed ecology

I stand by the claim I have made throughout the book that the premises around the parish, place and commitment to locality should not necessitate the conclusion that therefore the new churches are incongruous with the parish vocation. I simply cannot fathom how we have managed to create a divide within our ecclesial thinking between old and new, inherited and planted. If we are serious about the vocation to presence (that is, if we take seriously the cure of souls), then we must recognize the need for new things. I think what has happened is that because planting has been carried out mainly by evangelical churches and by evangelical churches of a particular flavour (for example, HTB), the conclusion has been drawn that starting new churches follows a different vocation within the Church of England. I think this is a shame, not least because my experience is that many of the churches planted by, say, HTB, have local engagement as their very *raison d'être*. But above all, it is a shame because it misses the potential for planting to serve the very vocation many critics are trying to protect. It is another example of where polarized and binary thinking has damaged our ability to reason well. It harms the work of planting activity, which is sidelined from the mainstream and thus given free space to think of planting in categories other than the cure of souls and presence (exactly what has happened), and it is detrimental to our inherited structures and systems, which miss out on the potential for planting to enhance the very thing many are longing for. To put it bluntly: Why can't it be that planting and grafting will be one of the ways in which the parish is 'saved'? To be clear: I am simply trying to create the ecclesiological space for new churches. What I cannot possibly claim is that every church that has been planted in the Church of England has been planted to serve the vocation to presence. Clearly this is not the case, and there has been (as with any new movement within an existing institution) a good amount of clumsiness in the way planting has been carried out, including in the articulation of its purpose. My claim is simply that, based on what I have argued thus far, if we are to be present to place, then we need to plant more parish churches, and we need to intentionally revitalize others that are at risk of becoming lost. The question then becomes, and not least in the light of how planting activity has been viewed up to this juncture: How might we do new churches well within this vocation to presence?

First, I do think that it is right that we ask how new churches are Church of England churches. I have checked myself many times on this, not least because as someone who leads front foot missiological (rather than, say, liturgical or doctrinal), I cringe when I hear others ask that same question of new churches. However, I do think it matters. Ultimately, of course, it matters because of integrity. However, the point I want to make here is that in addressing this issue we push into the vocation, with other issues of liturgical practice relativized accordingly. Thus, I suggest that in asking the question How is this a Church of England church? we think first about how this church is fulfilling the vocation of the cure of souls through presence in a definable place. Is it (essentially) being a congregational church, or is it somehow implicated in the life of the place it sits within? Perhaps the central question is: How does it define itself, and does this church imagine itself as existing for its place?

There are no simple guidelines to follow here, and the decisions that must be made are difficult. However, it does at least give some flavour of what the outcomes might be. For example, it seems to me that the Church of England might rightly be wary of starting a new church in, say, a warehouse in an out-of-town industrial estate. Again, this is not to devalue other churches for whom this is their God-given vocation. It is just to ask whether this really can or should be the Church of England's practice. If the vocation is right, then our instinct will be to start churches close to people, present in place rather than in space. To hold both the bounded *and* the open aspects of place together.

This issue taps into the wider conversation about Fresh Expressions and the early debates following *Mission-shaped Church* that I addressed above. As I say, my sense is that the initial pushback did express valid theological concerns about the relationship between Church of England churches and place. It did seem odd that the church would be so quick to embrace as a standardized model and strategy new non-placed churches (network churches, churches that exist for a particular social group, and – on the increase – online churches), given its vocation to presence. As others have pointed out, the issue primarily was the way in which that word 'church' seemed to be used: that these groups and projects were not simply vital missional activities, but were to be seen as church in their own right, distinctive from the parish church, and able to be fully Church of England churches without having, or being part of, an area of geographical responsibility. I'm not sure why we felt the need to do this. I think fresh expressions have a vital role to play within the mixed ecology of church; clearly they do, just as pioneer ministers have a role to play within and from out of our churches. The nature of place as bounded openness means that we will need multiple expressions of the church to be present in place. If the vision of the parish is to be for all, then we must find ways of connecting with those who would never come to the parish church building on (say) a Sunday morning. What I am arguing for here is that we see such expressions as a part of the place commitment of a church, or a group of churches. At the very least it seems right that such expressions are deliberately connected to the parish church(es) of that place.

The danger of the 'mixed ecology' language on this measure is that it too readily allows for a duality of vocations within the church, as though there were a way of being a Church of England church without the roles and responsibilities that come from being part of the body. My claim here is that not only does this step depend on insufficient ecclesiological foundations, but it is also unnecessary. A diversity of churches and expressions can (and I think should) exist as part of the one vocation: to be present to the places of the nation, bringing the church close to where people are. The 'mixed' must refer to expression rather than vocation. In this sense, fresh expressions, pioneer communities, house churches and new plants then fit within the vocation, as aspects (expressions) of the parish churches. The point is that they are a part of this common vocation to be present in this place.

The immediate question this poses is about how such variety is held within the whole. The goal must be to simultaneously uphold the integrity of the expression, alongside a sense of its catholicity (that this is not a solo enterprise but is a part of the local body in and for this place). My sense is that locality is the friend of catholicity in this respect; that being in the same shared (micro or macro) place, substantially connected with others, allows us to genuinely be one. In other words, we can speak of a parish church and its expressions, and we can do so with integrity because they are part of the one church in that place. Indeed, we might say that given the vocation of presence, locality should be the way that we conceive of catholicity in the Church of England. Inherited and new churches are one, not in the first place because they are part of the Church of England, but because they are part of the Church of England in this place.

On this note there has been a shift in recent years away from the language of Fresh Expressions and pioneering, towards language of starting new churches/church planting. There is lots going on here in terms of the culture within the Church of England. However, one way of looking at this shift is to see it as representative of the ecclesiology I have been outlining here. That is, a sense that church must take form as a visible and gathered public presence, rather than as an interest group or network. Again, I see such expressions as important; what we are observing, however, is that they are being run out of new 'churches' rather than as discrete entities. I think this is a positive shift.

Second, we need to be able to plant new parish churches in areas where there currently isn't a church presence. The fact is that many housing developments or new towns do not have a Church of England presence. To begin a new church here, therefore, is an act of presence in place. I have had the good fortune of working with a nearby plant, which was started on a new housing development in the newly built church primary school. What has been interesting is observing just how parish-like the planting ministry has been here. The ministers moved into the development and have spent time – collars on – walking round and meeting people, making connections; especially with the school community. There is now a congregation meeting every Sunday, which includes various groups meeting through the week in people's homes. If we plant such churches, then we need to be ready to alter boundaries, and make them legally a parish church for this new place. In many instances it would make sense to use the boundaries of the estate as the new parish boundary.

Third, what excites me about our current moment is that we are now seeing second- and third-generation church plants and grafts, which are therefore necessarily closer to micro places. This seems to me to be the logic of church multiplication;

eventually the process moves from a centre to the peripheries. It has been a shame that the conversation has been so defined by the response to large city-centre resourcing churches. As Nick Spencer argued a long time ago, the parish system should not be seen as opposed to such churches (Spencer uses the language of 'minster' churches, which I think is probably more helpful language than resource church); however, the impact of these takes some time.[11] The norm in church planting – and especially around the world today – is for smaller, rooted and deeply placed communities. My experience is that church planting occurs because of a hunger to be intentional, with little other output for this desire. I hope that if we prioritize presence in place and allow our structures to reflect this, we will find avenues for this desire that work within the structures. We need new churches, but we also need extraordinary entrepreneurial energy to enliven and reinvigorate existing ones.

One final word on the language of mixed ecology. There has been a development of the idea in recent years, with the original 'mixed economy' replaced by the now more organic metaphor. This move is itself representative of much that I have addressed in this book: economy holds all sorts of connotations associated with modern thinking, where ecology is suggestive of the organic, the given, the bound. As with all good metaphors, however, this one quickly becomes problematic and remains in ongoing need of nuancing. Ecology emphasizes the organic over the intentional: an ecosystem is necessarily chaotic; and equilibrium – when it does occur – emerges through competition rather than design.[12] The dangers of this thinking should be obvious to us: there are no apex predators in the church economy and survival of the fittest is not a worthy principle of ecclesiology. Indeed, a recognition that we have local churches that share together as one – particularity *and* catholicity – has been after all in many ways the defining feature of what we now call 'Anglican'. The original theological claim underpinning the Prayer Book and the other founding theologies is that it is credible to have a fully *local* church; that catholicity does not imply uniformity and that our sharing in Christ, which transcends time and space, must take local, particular form. In terms of our structures then, we need to recognize that we are one church in many different places. Mixed ecology language can imply that there are a variety of 'bodies' that are born and die (it is definitely the 'dying' part of the metaphor that we are less good at making sense of) alongside one another. Yet we are – all – one body of Christ, and thus have a responsibility to the other. This language of church as body is ultimately the one most true to the New Testament and Christian tradition, and is thus particularly important in our conversations about new churches; something argued for convincingly by the theologian Helen Morris.[13] What this means for those of us who are sold on the idea of new and old existing together is that we have to work to find ways for this relationship to be a genuine sharing in common life, rather than simply settling on an underdeveloped concept of 'different callings'. Once again, therefore, the question emerges, not whether planting or starting new things is right or wrong (a question that often relies on an assumed competition of resources; a scarcity mindset), but: *How do we do this well*? This must be answered on all sides. How is this process of starting new things and allowing other things to die well done in such a way that the whole body shares together? Diocesan strategy and (often more importantly) communications are sometimes poor in this regard and frequently invite a level of fear that always emerges in the space of silence. If we believe in what we are doing, then we must be prepared to say so; entirely transparent and inviting full participation. Where one part is lost for a season we must all feel it. And where a different part is flourishing, know that as our joy too.

My claim has been that the mixed ecology demanded by the nature of place demands a collegiality, and especially at the local levels: colleagues, ordained and lay, working with one another, supporting one another and sharing resources; believing the best of one another's intentions, responding in love rather than fear, and abundance rather than scarcity. This is a somewhat idealized vision I know, and the experience of so many of us is that this is difficult to achieve. There are significant differences in our traditions and commitments within this broad church, which make it very difficult to do this. To this I have one final comment.

It has been my experience that trust is built through relational encounter and sharing life. As we have seen, this itself is a feature of (good) presence in place: a movement away from idealized or imagined constructs, towards actual encounter and experience of the other. Unity is very difficult at systematic or macro-institutional levels. Unity becomes possible – in fact is obvious – when on the ground, in place, working in love. In this sense, locality is the friend of catholicity. I have often heard it said that 'This is all about the kingdom, not about empire building.' What I hope to have shown in this book is that the kingdom of God has very much to do with place; that the kingdom is not itself a place as much as the reality of God, which fills and completes every existing place. Might it be then that a shared commitment to a place could enable us to prioritize the kingdom together? What if our unity is best fostered in these local connections and a sharing in love for a place? In this sense a commitment to local place may become the richest way to conceive of our shared life. Sadly, the parish – which has been the given grammar for locality in the Church of England – has I think tended to work us away from this. The unwavering commitment to one's own place is ingrained into our imaginary, the unintentional by-product being that we tend to think in silo-like ways about our churches and their responsibility. If there is to be a renewed emphasis on the parish, then I hope we find ways to be local without being exclusionary; of moving towards the other in good faith rather than in fear. It is the nature of place to exist in relation to other places. No parish is an island, and there are enough souls for curing. Our shared commitment to this vocation may well be the best chance we have of holding together as one body.

Conclusion

I began this chapter by naming the problem of imagined presence and imagined coverage. Both are 'spatial' tendencies, a way of imposing some order or meaning or story on to a place. But the parish in its hopeful form has always been about engagement and encounter with what is there, about being close not simply in terms of proximity, but relationally. In this sense, the structure must serve this end, and a desire to sustain the structure might be the very thing preventing our engagement. One of the reasons we are drawn towards imagined coverage and presence is that genuine presence in place is, as we know, difficult. This is for many reasons but not least because – as our history shows – places change, and can never be neatly bounded; always a relationship of other places. Of course, every place is different. Where one place feels full of flux and change, another may feel static and settled. Thus, although the vocation is the same, the task is diverse. I hope to have shown, however, something of the character of such a task. It must be intentional, and at times strategic. It must account for the relationship between micro and macro. It becomes real at the church-congregational level, but demands something of us at diocesan and deanery levels: a work of the whole church. Finally, I argued that the vocation to presence should motivate rather than restrict the starting of new things. As I stated in the Introduction, a guiding conviction as I wrote this book was that we would do well to pay better attention to our instincts and refuse the tendency for these instincts to draw us into polarized positions. I hope that this final chapter has given some ground from which we can think about the place of new churches and new expressions: a way of holding together the old and the new. I think if we are to remain the church of and for the nation, then we need new things for new places, and we need new things for changing places. How we do all this is a different question, and I have only been able to give a flavour here. My prayer remains, however, that we might see a flourishing of inherited churches just as we might see many new churches started in our time. And new historic churches at that. Many of our new churches will of course be present in place for just a season – and this will be their gift to the Church of England and their place – but some will take root and become established. Breathed into life by the Spirit of God, and present to a place long into the future: perhaps even through the whole of the time that Christ has determined there to be.

Notes

1 Ingrid Leman Stefanovic, 2000, *Safeguarding our Common Future: Rethinking Sustainable Development*, New York: State University of New York Press, p. 116.

2 John Milbank, 'Stale Expressions: The Management-Shaped Church', *Studies in Christian Ethics*, 21:1 (2008), pp. 117–28.

3 The principle appeared in the House of Bishops' Pastoral Letter, 'Who is My Neighbour' at the 2015 General Election. See House of Bishops, 2015, 'A Letter from the House of Bishops to the People and Parishes of the Church of England for the General Election 2015', at https://www.churchofengland.org/sites/default/files/2017-11/whoismyneighbour-pages.pdf, accessed 03.04.2021.

4 See, for example, David Golemboski, 'Federalism and the Catholic Principle of Subsidiarity', *Publius: The Journal of Federalism*, 45:4 (2015), pp. 526–51. And John W. Bridge, quoted in Michelle Evans, 'The Principle of Subsidiarity as a Social and Political Principle in Catholic Social Teaching', *Solidarity: The Journal of Catholic Social Thought and Secular Ethics*, 3:1 (2013), pp. 44–60.

5 The historian Sheridan Gilley argues that pastoral provision was so focused on the rural south and Midlands that it was utterly unable to respond to the Industrial Revolution: 'The Church of England could be said to have lost the modern urban working class in the very decades of its formation.' Gilley, 1994, 'The Church of England 1800–1900', in *A History of Religion in Britain*, Sheridan Gilley and W. J. Shiels (eds), Oxford: Blackwell, pp. 291–305.

6 In Leeds, for example, by 1841 the parish church was serving over 150,000 people.

7 See Anthea Jones, 2000, *A Thousand Years of the English Parish*, Gloucester: Windrush, p. 268. The 1851 Religious Census revealed that there had been over 1,255 subdivisions of parishes and districts

up to that year. Jones argues that there was more to this than intended reorganization of ministry: 'The impetus for building churches came not so much from the Church as from Parliament, who saw the Church in its local form as a force to control social unrest' (p. 272). See also N. J. G. Pounds, 2004, *A History of The English Parish*, Cambridge: Cambridge University Press, p. 507.

8 In 1851, Richard Mann, who wrote the report on the Census of that year, argued that '[There is] no scheme for giving to a clergyman the cure of souls, within a small and definite locality, apart from the very onerous duties which attach to the possession of a church.' See Jones, *A Thousand Years*, p. 268. For Mann, therefore, it was not that the system itself was wrong, but rather that it needed applying in a particular way – specifically the move towards greater numbers of clergy working from one (larger) parish – if it was truly to allow the church to be what it desired to be. Likewise, the architect George Gilbert Scott argued in 1871 that the parochial system was being 'pushed to the extreme' (Jones, *A Thousand Years*, p. 283). It is important to note that in this period the church – in its parochial form – was not completely disconnected from communities but could be present in very rich ways. See, for example, Kenneth Hyslon-Smith, 1998, *The Churches in England from Elizabeth I to Elizabeth II*, vol. 3, London: SCM Press, pp. 65–9. And for a revision of the common assumption that the Anglican church 'lost' the working class, see Jeremy Morris, 2022, *A People's Church: A History of the Church of England*, London: Profile.

9 Minster Communities in the pattern agreed in the Diocese of Leicester in 2021. Mission areas offer a less substantive change and exist in a number of dioceses.

10 Andrew Rumsey, 2017, *Parish: An Anglican Theology of Place*, London: SCM Press, p. 67.

11 Nick Spencer, 2004, *Parochial Vision: The Future of the English Parish*, London: Paternoster Press.

12 In noticing the problem of ecosystem as competition, some have therefore spoken of a need for 'rewilding' the church, since rewilding is a process of encouraging nature to 'do its thing', but through careful land midwifery. This has been a popular concept for some fresh expressions, and pioneer thinkers and practitioners inside and outside the Church of England. See, for example, Steve Ainsthorpe, 2020, *Rewilding the Church*, Edinburgh: St Andrew Press.

13 Helen Morris, 2019, *Flexible Church: Being the Church in the Contemporary World*, London: SCM Press.

Postscript

Place and humility go hand in hand. To return to Willie James Jennings' claim, place is a mark of our creatureliness; a reminder that we are not God. Modern space thus establishes and perpetuates the sense that we have the power to control, to manipulate, to master. I wonder whether, therefore, it might be helpful to say that our conversations with one another in the church need to be marked more by place than by space. Place can only be understood from the inside. So too we must hear from the others' perspective, aware of our own projections of meaning. Place is about limit. So too we must recognize the horizon of our own experience; that what we have observed of the parish may not be what someone else has seen. Place is bounded and open. Thus, our conversations must be marked by the commitment to both what was and what is. If we let it, place might just shape our very thinking. We become marked by humility: the sympathetic mind.

I have been very wary in this book of offering too many explicit answers to the question of the parish today – as a result, perhaps, of my own fear of imposing from the outside. I recognize that this will have been frustrating for some readers. Ultimately, however, I make no apologies. For as I always say to my students in my mission classes, there is no silver bullet. I think sometimes we can pretend that there is one. Lots of books and articles have been written, a lot of seminars and talks given that seem to assume something like this. 'We've been doing x, but the thing we need to do is y.' So whether it is small groups, or house churches, or parish revival, or missional communities, or resourcing churches or whatever, we seem to find it very easy to slide from claiming something is good to believing it to be the answer. There are, however, two problems with this sort of silver-bullet thinking: God, and everything else. In terms of the latter, clearly the world is complex and so is the church. There are no easy solutions because the reality is not easy. Fallible humans make decisions. Structures are hard to shift. Though God is abundance, ledger sheets cannot be ignored. Further, as I suggested in the final chapter, when it comes to the parish, the issues we face go all the way up and all the way down. There is no easy answer or obvious culprit at the 'centre' of the church, just as there are no easy techniques that work in every place.

Second, however, God. I recently had to complete some Strategic Development Funding paperwork, and on the form it asked this question: 'What is your Theory of Change?' We really struggled to answer it. In the end, however, we simply wrote 'God'. Now, I dislike being seen to be facetious, so this didn't come naturally to me (I did go back later and explain what I meant…). But I really didn't know how else we are to answer that question as Christ's church. Surely, we must believe this to be the case? It is God who ministers, through his church. It is not our ministry; it has been entrusted to us by God and we partner with him in all he is doing in the world. Thus, if there is to be life, then it will be God who brings it, for without him there is no life, only darkness. In this sense, whatever our vocation might be, prayer and worship are our purpose. And if we do not do this – do not grow in holiness as a church, stop pursuing Christ as our singular goal, in other words stop giving God room to work through us – then no amount of changing the structure will ultimately matter. I hope I have shown enough in this book to underline that I do not think this is an excuse for passivity. God really has entrusted to us this vocation and has given us gifts. We cannot, therefore, dismiss the need for strategy and right management of resources. There are truly better or worse (more/less faithful) ways we might act. It is simply a restatement of one of the central themes of this book: that we need to be very careful not to mistake the gifts of God for God. I have argued that the Church of England has a vocation that originates in its charism, of being close to the places of the nation and being implicated in the life that happens in place. It is a vocation that resonates with the deep pull towards place; towards particularity, connection to the past, complexity and a sense of permanency. But it is a vocation that we receive as gift of God. This is the necessary corollary to the claim that we have a particular vocation to the parish, with which – necessarily – we are in danger of ecclesial arrogance. Yet if such arrogance is avoided it will not be because we have rejected the vocation, but because we have been on our knees to receive it from him alone (even as it comes to us through the medium of the state). The Lord gives and it is the Lord's to take away. The vocation is not eternal. If there is a conversation to be had about structures, therefore, then it must be marked by this type of humility. We will do our best to be faithful to what God has gifted us; to what we have received. But we will recognize that God is not finished, and will not be bound even to the means of his past working. There is no silver bullet. The Spirit blows where he wills.

This then is one way in which we might interpret Pope Gregory's dictum to the pioneering Saint Augustine as he arrived on these shores: 'For things are not to be loved for the sake of places, but places for the sake of good things.'[1] The parish system, as 'thing', is ultimately a means to the end of the *good* things – Christ's church finding him in place. When it becomes itself the object, we are in danger of losing these goods. A recovery of them will, as Gregory suggests, in part entail prising ourselves away from our misdirected loves and recovering a love of place. And as we love here, we might find the Good thing: him ahead of us at work in every place.

Notes

1 Bede, 1999, *Ecclesiastical History of the English People*, Judith McClure (trans.), Oxford: Oxford University Press, Book I section 27 part II.

Index